THE CRISIS OF KEYNESIAN ECONOMICS
A MARXIST VIEW

The Crisis of
Keynesian Economics

A MARXIST VIEW

Geoffrey Pilling

BARNES & NOBLE BOOKS
Totowa, New Jersey

© 1986 Geoffrey Pilling
First published in the USA 1986 by
Barnes & Noble Books,
81 Adams Drive,
Totowa, New Jersey, 07512

Library of Congress Cataloging in Publication Data applied for.
ISBN 0-389-20614-8

Printed and bound in Great Britain

CONTENTS

PREFACE

This book is a Marxist critique of certain aspects of Keynesianism. Whilst it concentrates on a review of Keynes' writings rather than the vast literature which has grown up amongst his followers over the last 40 years and more, it does pay some attention to the work of the 'left Keynesians' and in particular that of Joan Robinson. The fact that Keynesianism is manifestly in a crisis provided the opportunity to reconsider the nature of Keynes' contribution both to economic theory and economic policy. Many of the issues involved in such a review are perhaps now much clearer than they were in the long period after the war when Keynesianism ruled almost unchallenged in both the academic world as well as amongst the formulators of state economic and social policy.

Although written over a relatively short space of time, the themes of the book have concerned the author for some time. They arose in part from the fact that much of what passed for a Marxist treatment of Keynes was not only highly unsatisfactory but at the most fundamental level constituted a capitulation to the prevalent Keynesian orthodoxy. No doubt this unsatisfactory state of affairs had its roots in developments in the Soviet Union during the period in which Keynesianism first emerged and then gained a firm grip on the academic world. See Letiche (1971) for Soviet reactions to Keynes; they veered between a writing-off of his work as simply 'bourgeois' to serious concessions to his conceptions. As far as the Anglo-Saxon world is concerned, little attempt was made at a serious analysis of Keynesianism and this again can be attributed to the deleterious effect which Stalinism had on the development of Marxism over a long period. Some of this work is reviewed in what follows.

Yet for Marxism Keynesianism represented, and still represents, a serious challenge. In the first place it claimed to have resolved the fundamental problems of capitalism and to have provided the tools to put an end to capitalist crisis for good. More specifically, Keynes claimed to have dealt a deadly blow to Marxism, in particular to have knocked away its foundations which he saw as lying in the work of Ricardo. As such, Keynesianism became the ideology for various reformist currents in the working class, as well as for those who wished to pronounce Marxism in need of 'updating' to take account of the 'new phenomena' of modern capitalism (if indeed, post-Keynes, that term retained any meaning). It is true that the first claim, like reports of Mark Twain's death, can now be seen as perhaps somewhat exaggerated; as to the second claim, it rested essentially upon Keynes' ignorance of Marxism in general and of the latter's critique of political economy in particular. But to leave the matter there would be a mistake, if only because Keynesianism still retains a certain hold in sections of both the working class as well as amongst the intelligentsia. The programme of the Labour Party and TUC leadership put forward to deal with the current crisis (the so-called Alternative Economic Strategy) is essentially Keynesian in outlook, calling for the expansion of government expenditure as the means to cure a situation of chronic unemployment.

The book which follows is directed at those interested in Keynesianism and more generally in current questions of economic theory and policy. On a wider level though, it is written from the point of view that the development of Marxism takes place only in the systematic confrontation with all forms of bourgeois theory. It is not only inadequate merely to defend the integrity of Marxism in some formal sense: such a procedure must inevitably lead to dogmatism and sterility and ultimately to the abandonment of Marxism itself. There is no doubt that those many claiming to be Marxists who saw in post-war capitalism the opening-up of a new, essentially crisis-free phase in its development, drew their essential conceptions from Keynes' locker, even though their theories were clothed in Marxist-sounding terminology. In this camp I would certainly include those who saw in expenditure on armaments one of the principal instruments for capitalist stability. Under the same rubric can be placed those theories of neocapitalism which regarded the state as playing a decisive stabilising role in present-day capitalist economy.

These attempted revisions of Marxism involved by no means merely details of economic theory, but extended to the decisive questions of the Marxist world outlook and in particular its basic conception of the capitalist mode of production. It is for this reason that in considering Keynes' work I have concentrated on these issues.

Part of the contents of the book formed the basis for seminars in Middlesex Polytechnic in the academic year 1984–85 and I thank the students who participated in those discussions. I should also like to thank Len Gomes for the use he allowed me to make of his wide-ranging knowledge as well as for some helpful references in connection with Chapter 5. I make the statement, usual in these matters, that I alone am responsible for what follows.

ABBREVIATIONS

The following abbreviations have been used throughout the book:

I: *Capital*, vol. I (Lawrence & Wishart, London, 1961)

II: *Capital*, vol. II (Lawrence & Wishart, London, 1961)

III: *Capital*, vol. III (Lawrence & Wishart, London, 1961)

Th I, Th II, Th III *Theories of Surplus Value*, Parts 1–3, (Lawrence & Wishart, London)

GT: J.M. Keynes, *The General Theory of Employment, Interest and Money* (Macmillan, London, 1936)

JMK CW: *The Collected Writings of John Maynard Keynes* (Macmillan, London)

LCW: *The Collected Works of Lenin* (50 vols) (Lawrence & Wishart, London)

MECW: *The Collected Works of Marx and Engels* (Lawrence & Wishart, London)

DR: *The Works of David Ricardo*, ed. Sraffa, Cambridge University Press, Cambridge

REACTIONS TO THE CRISIS OF KEYNESIANISM

There are still echoes of the debate, now well past its centenary, between Marxists and neoclassical economists, but not much of this is heard anywhere in professional circles, and there is certainly very little in it to exercise the general body of economic practitioners. Economics seems, miraculously, to have ceased to be the battleground of conflicting ideologies. As we shall see, there are many and sometimes very profound differences of view on particular issues, especially where specific points of economic policy are concerned. But, while it may be going too far (paraphrasing Sir William Harcourt) to say 'we are all Keynesians now', it seems that in our analytical moments most economists are prepared to take the innovations of Keynes and his disciples for granted. (Roll 1968: vi–vii)

Virtually everybody is prepared to agree that a deep malaise now afflicts the once seemingly omnipotent Keynesian political economy. Many are of the opinion that we have already seen the end of the Keynesian era. But there is little agreement amongst orthodox economists about the nature of this illness, its origin and the means to its cure, assuming that it is not in fact terminal. This book attempts, from a Marxist standpoint, to examine various facets of the crisis pervading Keynesianism and thereby provide a critique of Keynesian economics. This it does because, however severe their predicament, Keynesian ideas still retain an important influence, not least in the British labour movement. Thus in the so-called Alternative Economic Strategy — proposed by the Trades Union Congress and others in opposition to the economic policies pursued by the Thatcher governments since 1979 — a large element of Keynesianism is clearly visible. This opening chapter surveys this crisis, outlines several reactions to it from economists and others, and in so doing sketches out the major themes of the book.

It is almost universally accepted that the capitalist economic system is currently experiencing its most acute crisis since the 1930s. Following the end of the Second World War in 1945, a quarter century of boom, interrupted by relatively shallow and localised recessions in the major capitalist countries, suddenly erupted into the violent inflation of the early 1970s, subsequently to collapse into a global slump which, judged by the standards of the post-war years, remains unprecedented in its severity and duration. An important casualty of this crisis has been Keynesian political economy, the severe illness or even death of which has been either celebrated or lamented at various points of the political compass.

According to the conventional view of the history of economic theory, until the 1930s it had been confidently held by the majority of economists that the smooth expansion of capitalism's productive forces would, on the whole, assure conditions of economic stability, growth and full employment. Unemployment was usually considered to be the responsibility of market 'imperfections', especially those connected with wage rigidities. Any persistent unemployment was held to be due to the unwillingness of workers to accept a wage level that would 'clear the market'. It was the slump of the 1920s and 1930s which threw this economic theory (designated by Keynes as 'classical' economics) into a severe crisis. Keynes emerged as the principal figure who attempted to explain this economic crisis and tried to chart a course out of it. The result was Keynesian economics which emerged as the standard economic theory of the postwar world, exercising a powerful intellectual dominance until the very recent past. Thanks to this new economics, it was widely accepted that given an appropriate manipulation of the budgetary aggregates and suitable monetary policies, what Keynes was to term the level of effective demand could be raised to a point where all involuntary unemployment was more or less eliminated.

Writing of the decade following the end of the war, J.K. Galbraith said, 'Within a decade [after 1945] the belief that the modern economy was subject to a deficiency in demand — and that offsetting government action would be required — was close to becoming the new orthodoxy' (Galbraith 1973: 189).

Keynes and Radicalism

Now whether this Keynesian-type policy was ever in fact practised after 1945, and whether, if practised, it was responsible for the sustained period of expansion from the end of the war onwards are moot points. Many commentators are doubtful about both these propositions. But one fact is beyond dispute: if not as an economic policy certainly as an ideology, Keynesianism exercised a powerful influence after 1945. On the left especially it was generally assumed that, thanks to Keynes' discoveries in economic theory, a social-political crisis of the sort which had broken out with such catastrophic consequences in the 1930s was now largely a thing of the past. In particular, Keynesianism had provided the answer to a Marxism which had made such ground amongst the younger intelligentsia in the 'red decade' of the 1930s. Calling *The General Theory* 'the most influential book on economic and social policy this century', Galbraith was certainly not out on a limb when he declared that 'By common, if not yet quite universal agreement, the Keynesian revolution was one of the great modern accomplishments in social design. It brought Marxism in the advanced countries to a total halt' (Galbraith 1971: 43–4).

So confident was Galbraith in the victory of Keynesianism that he could bemoan the fact that the 'old' microeconomic problem in economics — the allocation of scarce resources amongst competing ends — had been forced largely off the agenda with the consequence that key problems, notably the contradiction between public wants and private needs, was now seriously neglected.

Such ideas exercised a considerable influence in Britain in the 1950s and 1960s, not least in Labour Party circles where a wing of the party emerged declaring that Marxism was now discredited and out-of-date, and demanding that an even nominal commitment to socialist aims, embodied in clause 4 of the party constitution, be ditched. The impact of the prevailing Keynesian orthodoxy could be measured in a series of influential books by writers such as Anthony Crosland, by the former Marxist, John Strachey, and others extolling the virtues of the new post-war capitalism which, thanks to Keynes, had overcome its proneness to crises and thereby rendered Marxism obsolete. As Stuart Holland declared:

> Keynes was not a socialist, and was almost wholly ignorant of the work of the founding-father of modern socialism — Marx. Yet he had more influence on post-war British socialists than any other theorist of our time. It is also arguable that, almost single-handed, he buried Marxism for a generation of the mainstream British left. (Skidelsky (ed.) 1977: 67)

It is easy to see what attracted radical thought towards Keynesianism. Keynes was in favour of limited measures of social reform. He doubted the efficacy of unaided monetary control. A trenchant defender of private property, he none the less held that the 'socialisation of investment' would serve to make capital abundant and thus force down the interest rate eventually to zero, perhaps within the space of 25 years. While private capital would continue, the claims of *rentier* capital would be destroyed. The resulting scene was a Fabian-type world in which the grosser inequalities of wealth were to be removed by fiscal means (Keynes supported a 'moderately conservative' degree of income redistribution as one way of boosting consumption) where no reward is extracted by 'unproductive' capital and where employment is preserved at or near its maximum by the manipulation of state investment. It is little wonder that with some justice Keynes could be hailed as the new post-war apostle of social democracy.

On the basis of this type of conception a general consensus emerged. Capital left unregulated might still prove crisis-prone, but given suitable social and economic state policies any instabilities could be kept within politically acceptable limits. Keynes, it seemed, had assured capitalism's future, albeit a somewhat different capitalism from the *laissez-faire* type which had existed for much of the nineteenth century. Politics could now occupy the middle ground, concerning itself with the balance of measures to be followed to achieve generally accepted aims within the framework of a beneficent welfare capitalism.

Some, of course, went further, denying that in the age of Keynes any meaningful use could be made of the term capitalism. We now lived in the era of post-industrial society, to use the term favoured by the American sociologist, Daniel Bell. Others preferred the notion of industrial society, still others that of technocratic society. Whatever differences existed between such conceptions, they were united in declaring Marxism to be outmoded, a doctrine at best a reflection of those nineteenth-century conditions which had now thankfully disappeared.

While a minority of radical economists such as Galbraith resented the fact that economics appeared to have little room for judgements about economic choice — he pointed to the increasing public squalor which the growth of private wealth appeared to entail — others positively welcomed the fact that social problems, or rather problems which had hitherto been considered social, were now taking on a purely technical form, concerning, in essence, the matter of the most efficient ('economic') allocation of human and material resources to satisfy social and personal needs. Economics had at last come of age. Invested with considerable prestige because of its seeming ability after Keynes to resolve hitherto intractable problems, its procedures were becoming more and more rigorous, employing mathematical techniques, and aspiring to the precision and methods which were assumed to guide the physical sciences. Economics could look down with a certain disdain at the still-infant social sciences. Eric Roll summed up this comparatively new and happy state of affairs:

> For some thirty years after the appearance of Keynes' *General Theory* the status of economics, largely associated with his general approach,

increased steadily until it reached a position of authority, both as a branch of social science and as a tool for the better solving of human affairs, unparalleled in its history and unequalled by any of the non-physical sciences. (Roll 1973: 548)

The leading, almost unchallenged, position occupied by Keynesianism undoubtedly left its imprint on Marxism. There were those Marxists who accepted the new economics of Keynes and believing that capitalism had indeed resolved its fundamental problems — at least in the economic sphere — turned their main attention elsewhere: to the residual cultural problems which were still held to afflict capitalism. Here was an international trend, finding a variety of expressions: the work of the Frankfurt school; in America that of Herbert Marcuse and in Britain in the New Left. One result of such tendencies was a turn away from a study of Marx's work in economics as found in *Capital* in favour of Marx the 'humanist' and 'philosopher' as exemplified in the *Paris Manuscripts* of 1844, with their theme of alienation. Not only did this artificially divide Marx's work along quite unwarranted lines but it also meant that Marxists tended in their work to reflect the increasing fragmentation of the social sciences, each engaged in their hermetically-sealed compartments.

On a narrower plane, those Marxists who did continue work in the sphere of political economy were also often influenced by the prevailing Keynesian conventional wisdom in that they were now inclined to believe that certain forms of state action could iron out the cyclical tendencies within capitalism. This in turn led some of them to read Marx's *Capital* through the prism of one variant or other of underconsumptionism. By underconsumptionism is meant the view, shared by a variety of writers in the history of economics including Malthus and J.A. Hobson, that a state of stagnation is not simply a passing phase of the capitalist economic cycle, nor the result of a momentary and fortuitous conjuncture of forces, but is a condition towards which the economy spontaneously tends in the absence of counteracting forces, including (for some at any rate) appropriate state action. We leave aside for the moment the question whether Keynes' *General Theory* can legitimately be considered to lie within the tradition of underconsumptionism. There is no doubt, however, that underconsumptionism was the basis for the stagnationist thesis popular immediately after the end of the war and advanced by a number of economists who, particularly in America, emerged as Keynes' leading advocates and interpreters. (In Joseph Schumpeter's opinion, 'Keynes may be credited or debited, as the case may be, with the fatherhood of modern stagnationism' (Schumpeter 1963: 1172).) Alvin Hansen was one of the leading proponents of the view that the major problem likely to face capitalism after 1945 was that of stagnation. But it was a view about the essential problem facing capitalism by no means confined to these Keynesian circles. To take but one example. A work such as Baran and Sweezy's *Monopoly Capital* which appeared in the mid-1960s saw capitalism's central problem as being associated not with its inability to extract surplus value but with the generation of a surfeit of surplus value. Thanks to the ability of the monopolists to manipulate their prices, more surplus value was created than could possibly be accumulated and this required ever greater and irrational expenditures on the part of the state which would 'waste' this excess surplus. A variant on this essentially underconsumptionist theme was the view which held that capitalism's post-war stability rested on a rising arms budget which had provided an effective leak for a growing volume of surplus value and had allowed capitalism to escape the consequences of the law which Marx had regarded as the most fundamental of all: the law of the tendency of the rate of profit to fall. This position was the basis of those theories which went under the name of the 'permanent arms economy'.

As is now obvious, the theory of a crisis-free 'transformed' capitalism proved, to say the least, to be somewhat optimistic. The once virtual unanimity amongst economists and politicians about the benign results to be obtained from the employment of Keynesian-type policies has now been shattered, many would hold irrevocably so. Near-rampant inflation in the early 1970s combined with a collapse of industrial production and employment in many ways surpassing the decline seen in the period after 1929 defy the central logic of Keynesianism where such things are not supposed to happen simultaneously.[1] In a recent lecture, Sir Charles Carter asked somewhat plaintively 'What is Wrong with Keynes?' (Carter 1981). He pointed out that in the 1960s, according to the precepts of Keynesianism, in a situation of slump the government would — within the constraints imposed by the balance of payments situation — have raised spending and cut taxes. Now precisely the opposite was happening. And Carter rightly drew attention to the fact that this was not a policy confined to the Thatcher government, the result of some abberant ideology as it were, for in the face of rising unemployment and inflation similar policies were pursued by the Wilson–Callaghan governments of 1974–79. Indeed it was James Callaghan, then prime minister, who warned the Labour Party Conference of 1976 that it was no longer possible to spend one's way out of a slump as far as he was concerned, pronouncing the death sentence on traditional Keynesianism:

We used to think that you could spend your way out of a recession, and increase employment by cutting taxes and boosting government expenditure. I tell you in all candour that that option no longer exists, and that in so far as it ever did exist, it only worked on each occasion since the war by injecting a bigger dose of inflation into the economy, followed by a higher level of employment as a next step.

Because of its chronic weakness, the British economy of the 1960s had already anticipated a crisis which was to assume international proportions in the following decade. The mid-1960s saw a series of savage deflationary measures carried out by a Labour government at the behest of the International Monetary Fund which had singularly failed to correct a long-standing balance of payments problem. The failure of these measures eventually forced the 1967 sterling devaluation, which in turn resulted in a series of severe disturbances in the world gold and currency markets. The end result was the decision taken by the American administration in August 1971 to remove gold backing from the dollar, a measure which had sustained the post-war Bretton Woods monetary arrangements for the previous 25 years or so. It is this economic crisis, with its attendant political and social implications, which has plunged both economic theory and the formulation of economic policy into a crisis. In its scope and depth, this crisis certainly promises to eclipse that of the 1930s. John Hicks, a leading interpreter of Keynes from the time of *The General Theory* (1936) onwards, holds that the current problems of Keynesianism present one of the gravest questions with which the world is now confronted (Hicks 1974).

Certainly not all share Hicks' sombre attitude. Some hope that a new Keynes will somehow emerge to resolve our current theoretical and practical problems; meanwhile Micawber-like we should muddle along with whatever tools are to hand. Others have suggested that there is little fundamentally wrong with orthodox economic theory. Our malaise stems from the fact that there is a widespread over-concern with theory as such. What is required is not more theory but better, more reliable, data on which to base rational economic policies. Viewed from this angle, the problems we face turn on a faulty division of labour amongst economists between theoretical and applied work.

But for those who still attach central importance to matters of economic theory, and who are concerned with the Keynesian crisis, there is little agreement about (a) the real significance of Keynes' contribution to economics, and (b) its contemporary relevance. Any Marxist view of Keynes must tackle both of these questions. Here, as an introduction, we summarise a range of answers to these questions from various non-Marxist standpoints.

The Monetarist Counter-Revolution

One group which in a certain sense stands outside the major disputes surrounding Keynesianism is the Austrian school of economics, deriving its inspiration from the work of Hayek and Ludwig von Mises. (Lionel Robbins' work (1932) was an expression of its influence amongst certain English economists.) Hayek has of course been a life-long opponent of socialism and of any schemes consciously to manage society, and this he justifies through the view of the market as an information system making it possible to use the economic information scattered amongst an enormous number of production agents. Hayek was one of the most determined of Keynes' opponents and for a short period his theory was regarded as a possible alternative to the new economics. According to Hayek, responsibility for the critical situation which the western economies currently face rests not with capitalism as such but with long-standing erroneous monetary and fiscal policies which stemmed from the influence of Keynesianism. Hayek and the Austrians generally regard as faulty the Keynesian explanation of involuntary unemployment as being due to a lack of effective demand. In reality it is caused by a series of imbalances between supply and demand in the labour markets of particular sectors of the economy. Full employment can be restored only on the basis of the adjustment of prices and wages in each individual sector of the economy, so that supply and demand are once again in equilibrium. In other words, Hayek is an advocate of the old idea of wage-cutting as a cure for unemployment, a policy which Keynes had supposedly laid to rest many years ago. For Hayek it is the Keynesian policy of stimulating demand to combat unemployment which has led to inflation. In his ideal economy prices are stable but wages flexible, the budget is in balance and the state has lost its monopoly right to issue money, with its role as provider of employment severely reduced. Austrian economics is a school based on extreme individualism and a pronounced anti-empiricism. This has led the Austrians to a deep suspicion not of Keynesian macroeconomics as such, but rather to the possibility of arriving at any macroeconomic aggregates such as consumption, investment, national income or a general index of prices. Because each individual agent in the economic process is unique, the attempt to sum the activities of such individuals is futile. In this respect Hayek and company attack the 'neoclassical synthesis' from a position diametrically opposed to that of the post-Keynesians. It is not Keynesianism which has made unwarranted concessions to the neoclassical orthodoxy but quite the reverse, the neoclassicists, by embracing the sort of macro-aggregates which Keynesianism implied, have seriously compromised their principles.

From the point of view of its ideological role and the sort of economic policy it proposes, monetarism — whose central figure is Milton Friedman — has however been a far more significant line of criticism of Keynesian orthodoxy than that provided by the Austrians. In essence, monetarism involves the call for a return to some version or other of a 'sound' pre-Keynesian economic theory. On the left especially it was widely expected that without radical government intervention in the economy the end of the Second World War would bring at best a period of chronic stagnation or at worst an outright collapse of the economy. For reasons to be discussed later (Chapter 4) this was not the case and inflation gradually emerged as a central economic and political problem. It was under the impact of such inflationary pressures, and especially as they began to mount dramatically in the 1970s, that monetarism emerged as the new and fashionable 'counter-revolutionary' doctrine.

Friedman was a prominent figure amongst the minority of post-war economists who refused to go along with the remedies for the ills of capitalism supported by Keynes and his followers. Not only was he an opponent of the sort of state intervention advocated by Keynes, but he advanced a quite different explanation for the slump of the 1930s which had led to the writing of *The General Theory*. On one not insignificant point Friedman did however agree with Keynes: the 1929 crash could have been avoided. But for Friedman the slump was generated not by an inadequate level of government spending or an unwillingness to borrow, but by the Fed's failure to provide adequate liquidity for the banking system. When the downturn began, following the Wall Street collapse, the Fed should have allowed an increase in the money supply. Instead it did precisely the opposite and as a result bank failures multiplied and a general collapse ensued.[2]

According to Friedman the 'real' economy is fundamentally sound. Any malfunctioning it experiences is engendered by disturbances in the monetary sphere. (From an historical point of view, Friedman was here saying nothing essentially new in that there had long been a strain in orthodox economics which had invoked monetary disturbances as the basis for their theories of dislocations within the capitalist economy, hardly surprising in view of the fact that money is the connecting link in all economic transactions and that the state, through the Central Bank, can vary the supply of money and credit.) Friedman has attempted to show that changes in the monetary stock have preceded great turning-points in the cyclical movement of the economy and that the central condition for economic stability is a sound monetary policy which acts not upon interest rates but on the money supply. For Friedman monetary policy is the decisive instrument for the regulation of the exchange rate, the price level, the nominal level of national income and, through changes in the money supply, the rate of inflation and deflation.

The influence which the ideas of the monetarists have enjoyed in the recent past undoubtedly stems in part at least from their apparent simplicity: the control of one variable in the economic system (the money supply) offers the key to the regulation of all others. But whether Friedman's ideas provide a key to understanding the crisis of contemporary capitalism is an entirely different matter, as we shall see. [3]

Even on the level of what monetarism takes to be its strongest point — its correspondence with 'the facts' — considerable doubt now surrounds Friedman's work. Thus in a recent article published by the Bank of England, it has been suggested that Friedman has severely manipulated his data in order to establish the central proposition of monetarism, namely that changes in the money supply have a close and causal connection with the rate of price inflation. Monetarism is founded upon the well-known Fisher equation, $MV = PT$: the supply of money (M) multiplied by the velocity of its circulation (V) is equal to the price level (P), multiplied by the number of transactions in the given period (T). But monetarism goes on to claim that because V and T are relatively stable, the equation can be reduced to one where $M = P$. Now in this examination of Friedman's major work by a noted econometrician (Hendry 1983) it has been discovered, for instance, that Friedman has reduced the money stock figures by 20 per cent for the years 1921–55 (which amounts to nearly one-third of the span of his studies) on the ground that war and depressions cause people to hold more money than in normal times. Similarly Friedman boosts the post-war price level to allow for price controls and rationing: he argues that the price level must have been higher than official statistics reveal since the money supply grew more rapidly than prices. Hendry then shows that the Nobel prizewinner uses his modified data to substantiate his central thesis: that the movement of prices depends on the movement of the money supply, the clearest case of circular reasoning. In short, Hendry suggests that Friedman's propositions are assertions without empirical basis.

This book will not be centrally concerned with the claims of the monetarists. [4] But in any event Eric Roll's sanguine view that there was near unanimity amongst economists on the fundamental problems of economic theory and that most accepted the tenets of Keynesianism no longer holds. For not only has Keynesianism come under fire from the Chicago school, it has also been attacked from a variety of different angles. For some, it seems, the Keynesianism which predominated after 1945 had little to do with the genuine article found in the writings of Keynes himself.

Bastard Keynesianism?

Professor Hutchison is amongst those who object that in the post-war world a pseudo-Keynesianism was practised which had little connection with the original teaching of Keynes. Keynesian doctrine became a dogma which was used to justify policies of expansion and growth, with little regard being paid for the cost of such measures. He sees four elements in this false Keynesianism. First, policies were pursued by governments which drove the level of unemployment below a figure considered by Keynes to be safe. Second, strategies of growth in accordance with maximum potential ('full growth') were followed and this became the overriding aim of economic policy. On the other hand, price stability was accorded little importance. Any tendency towards inflation was to be combatted by wages policies. For each of these positions, Hutchison finds little support in Keynes' writings. In support of this contention he has drawn attention to a series of articles written by Keynes in 1937 which opposed the idea that the threat of another slump could be averted by more government spending. Hutchison summarises his argument as follows:

> It is the pressing claims of a wide range of policy objectives, or the fact that throughout much of the post-war period the British economy has been on, or pretty near, a kind of policy-making frontier . . . which constitutes such a complete contrast with the policy situations which confronted Keynes in the inter-war years. Keynes made the point that when one moves from conditions of unemployment to those of full employment a number of theoretical and policy propositions which held in one case cease to hold in the other. . . . Policy problems certainly take on a very different and more complex form when one moves from an economy averaging 14 per cent unemployment . . . to one averaging 1.5 to 2.5 per cent. (Hutchison 1968)

One effect of Hutchison's work is to devalue the whole concept of the Keynesian revolution, certainly as far as its implications for policy are concerned. He suggests that amongst professional economists at any rate there was a wide measure of agreement about economic policy in the late 1920s and early 1930s. With one or two notable exceptions (concentrated at the LSE) virtually all economists, whatever differences of a theoretical character separated them, and whatever their economic theory suggested, were opposed to wage-cutting as a means of reducing unemployment under the specific conditions then prevailing. This is true particularly of Professor Pigou who, argues Hutchison, must be exculpated from the widespread charge that he was an advocate of wage reductions to resolve the crisis of the 1930s. Hutchison is one economist who doubts whether any real significance can be given to the term 'classical economics', again as far as policy questions are concerned. Here are raised a series of problems about the place of Keynes in the history of economics and about the true character of the Keynesian revolution, matters to which we turn in the next chapter.

Hutchison's 'pseudo-Keynesians' include the members of the Cambridge school, the leading figure amongst whom for many years was Joan Robinson. Now, ironically, Joan Robinson, like Hutchison, is of the opinion that the Keynesianism which emerged in the post-war world was not the genuine article: she has scathingly termed it 'bastard' Keynesianism. But her view as to what constituted genuine Keynesianism is far different from that proposed by Hutchison, itself an indication of the advanced state of disintegration prevailing in economics. Robinson's complaint boils down to the fact that what were passed off as Keynesian techniques — techniques which she believes were used to keep the capitalist system going after the war — actually obscured the real revolutionary character of Keynes' thought. Keynesianism was married to a discredited and ideologically bankrupt neoclassical economics and was thereby transformed into a new form of apologetics.

The version of Keynes reproduced in countless textbooks to which Robinson and others take such exception can be summarised as follows. It views the economy as rather like a machine; it consists of a series of flows, the relationship between which is highly stable, in principle knowable and therefore also in principle predictable from previous experience. Should one economy-wide flow fail to occur at an appropriate rate, the deficiency can be repaired by the government's intervention and regulation of those flows over which it does have direct control — the levels of taxation and public spending. There are known, stable relationships between government spending and income (and by extension, employment): by appropriate manipulation of such flows the volume of employment may be adjusted in line with policy objectives. Thomas Balogh captures the flavour of the line of criticism emanating from the radical Keynesians when he says of what became known pejoratively as 'hydraulic Keynesianism',

> . . . a new theoretical edifice was erected which would be reconnected to the neoclassical theory of harmony and just shares in the distribution of income. The old optimism about this being the best (and just) world was reasserted. The classical automatism of the market economy, maintaining full employment and ensuring optimal allocation of resources was just replaced by the *deus ex machina* consisting of the Treasury and the Central Bank. . . . The new self-consistent and determinate system was completed by the idea that politicians could choose at their discretion the level of unemployment — from a menu served up by econometricians — and that this level would be an expression of the will of the community and depend on how much inflation they were prepared to tolerate. (Balogh in Thirwall (ed.) 1974: 83–4)[5]

Post-Keynesianism

Balogh is here reflecting the views of a trend which became known as neo-Keynesianism or post-Keynesianism (in general the latter term will be employed in this book). It was a trend or school which objected to the standard income–expenditure model or orthodox textbook version of *The General Theory*, opposed, that is, to those who read that work through the eyes of general equilibrium theory. Now on this latter point, and despite the claims of the post-Keynesians, *The General Theory* certainly does contain many statements to the effect that with the establishment of full employment, the laws of general equilibrium come into operation and the economy then functions along lines suggested by neoclassical theory; furthermore such a position of general equilibrium could be re-established by means of fiscal and monetary policy. Here was the basis for the marriage of Keynesianism and the old neoclassical theory to produce the neoclassical synthesis which in turn provided the justification for the notion of the 'mixed economy' and government intervention. From the mid-1960s onwards, however, a new generation of Keynesians emerged critical of these traditional interpretations, among them Clower, Leijonhufvud, Paul Davidson and Sydney Weintraub. Their principal object of attack was the view of Keynes proposed by Hicks, Hansen,

Samuelson and others. Clower, for instance, argued that Keynes' theory was more than anything a theory of disequilibrium, a theory depicting an economy that did not seek to re-establish equilibrium but continually to upset it. According to Clower, such instabilities arise from imperfect information, from the difference in expected and realised magnitudes, factors which are potential sources of chain-reactions in the economy and which ceaselessly undermine its steady state. Leijonhufvud, like Clower, held that Keynes' theory cannot be reduced to a particular case of equilibrium because there is, in point of fact, no equilibrium; disturbances to the economy are not accidental but organic, the results of uncertainty, imperfections in economic information and the inelastic economic responses to various changes. This stress on uncertainty and lack of information is connected with the critique of the notion of perfect competition, a critique with which the name of Sraffa was closely associated from the 1930s onwards.

Weintraub (1979) provides a list of the major objections which this school holds against orthodox Keynesianism. First, it oversimplifies the nature of the economy and suggests that it can experience either inflation or unemployment, but not both simultaneously. Second, it pays little attention to the importance of price changes in the functioning of the economy. Third, it largely ignored uncertainty and inadequate information as determinants of the level of investment. Fourth, orthodox Keynesianism abstracted from the problems of distribution and thus laid the basis for an unwarranted split between macro- and microeconomics. Fifth, it misinterpreted Keynes' theory as being one concerned with the economy in a state of rest, whereas it was in essence dynamic.

Of all the writers who have stressed this question of the inherent unknowability of the future and the consequences of this fact for economic theory, G.L.S. Shackle has been the outstanding figure and described by one writer (Loadsby 1976) as the only genuine Keynesian. This is how Shackle views the efforts of orthodox Keynesianism to wed the old equilibrium economics to *The General Theory*:

In the later 1920s and the 1930s a great spasm of creative effort in economic theory responded to the visible dissolution of the comparatively orderly Victorian world in which Marshall had been able to discern the gradual perfectibility of industrial and social organisation hinting at the perfectibility of human nature itself. The tranquility had been shattered, and the theory of economic life which reflected it needed to be transcended and even wholly subverted. Not merely the detailed design of the economist's account of things needed to be changed, but its fundamental assumptions, its purposes and ambitions, what it claimed to do had to be essentially reconsidered. Such a reorientation was hard to accept and is still mainly unaccepted. (in Weintraub 1979: 37)

As we have noted, in stressing the role of disequilibrium and uncertainty, the critics of the orthodox reading of Keynes point to the financial instability of the capitalist economic system: uncertainty produces fluctuations in the economy precisely because of its elaborate system of monetary and financial institutions which are especially vulnerable to change under the impact of pessimistic or optimistic expectations.

This is the theme of a book published in the mid-1970s which provides a 'left' interpretation of Keynesianism by the American economist Professor Hyman Minsky (Minsky 1976). Like Balogh, Minsky deeply resents the fact that the Keynesian revolution was aborted in the period after the last war. He too holds that 'the integrated Keynesian classical economic theory — what is labelled the neoclassical synthesis — does violence to both the spirit and substance of Keynes' work' (ix). He goes on in the following vein about *The General Theory*:

the work contains the seeds for a deep intellectual revolution in economics and in the economist's view of society. However these seeds never reached their full fruition. The embryonic scientific revolution was aborted as the book's ideas were interpreted and analysed by academics and then applied by these same academics as a guide to public policy. (Minsky 1976: 4)

Like some of the Cambridge school Keynesians, Minsky stresses the inherent instability of capitalism, the fact that decision-making necessarily takes place under conditions of uncertainty and that financial relations and institutions play a central role in its functioning. And it was because Keynes saw these issues as central that his book, far from being dead, has great relevance, provided that it is interpreted in the correct spirit. So

in the neglected facets of *The General Theory* there is a theory of the processes of a capitalist economy that is much more appropriate for problems of economic analysis and policy now confronting us than is contained in the standard economic theory. (ibid.)

Keynes and Classical Political Economy

Now the implications of Minsky's approach to the general message of *The General Theory* and its continuing significance for the current problems of capitalist economy is important not merely for economic policy but for an assessment of Keynes' real place in the development of economic theory. Joan Robinson has been in the vanguard of those insisting that Keynesian economics, properly interpreted, belongs not to the neoclassical but the the classical tradition represented by Adam Smith and above all by David Ricardo. This is so because Keynes, like Smith and Ricardo, was concerned with economic aggregates. The typical neoclassical problem as formulated in a long line of writings from Jevons onwards, was one concerned with the process whereby a given income was allocated in the most rational manner. By rejecting the proposition that one could start from a given, full-employment, level of national income, and by focusing on those forces which determined both the level and the fluctuations of national income, Keynes was, according to the Cambridge school, posing the type of question asked by the classical economists: Under what conditions can an abundance of commodities be assured? Thus, says Robinson,

> By making it impossible to believe any longer in automatic reconciliation of conflicting interests into a harmonious whole, the *General Theory* brought out into the open the problem of choice and judgement that the neoclassicals had managed to smother. The ideology to end all ideologies broke down. Economics once more became political economy. (Robinson 1962: 76)

Eric Roll largely agrees with Robinson's judgement:

> The opinion may therefore be ventured that Keynes' approach represents, above all, a return to the preoccupations of classical political economy, and to that extent a departure from that concentration upon the implications of individual choice which had so long been the distinguishing characteristic of the central part of modern economic theory. It is such a departure in economic methodology in general, rather than as merely a contribution to the study of economic fluctuations, that the Keynesian system acquires its greatest significance. (Roll 1973: 486)

Robinson is, if anything, prepared to go further. For Keynes' overall approach constituted a return not merely to the traditions of the classical economists but at the same time to those of Marx:

> Academic theory, by a path of its own, has arrived at a position which has considerable resemblance to Marx's system. In both unemployment plays an essential part. In both capitalism is seen as carrying within itself the seed of its own decay. On the negative side, as opposed to the orthodox equilibrium theory, the systems of Keynes and Marx stand together, and there is now for the first time, enough common ground between Marx and Keynes to make discussion possible. (Robinson 1951: 137)

For Marxism these are obviously serious matters. They raise critical questions about Keynes' place in the evolution of economic thought, in particular his relationship to the classical–Marxian tradition and about his methodological innovations in the subject. We shall examine each of these matters (Chapter 3) by means of a consideration of the methodological foundations of Keynes' work.

Joan Robinson and other members of the Cambridge school have stressed an element which they see underpinning much of Keynes' work, namely the emphasis which it gives to the inherent uncertainty implicit in all economic processes. This uncertainty arose from the fact that economic events occur through time, which means that it is in principle impossible to predict the future on the basis of past experience. This is how Robinson makes the point:

> When Keynes was writing *The General Theory* his main difference from the school from which he was struggling to escape lay in the recognition of effective demand, which they ignored. It was for this reason that he put everyone from Ricardo to Pigou into one category, and for this reason that he overvalued Malthus. After the book was published, he drew the line differently. He saw that the main distinction was that he recognised, and they ignored, the obvious fact that expectations of the future are necessarily uncertain. It is from this point of view that post-Keynesian theory takes off. The recognition of uncertainty undermines the traditional notion of equilibrium. (preface to Eichner 1979)

Shackle also wishes to stress a similar point. Commenting on the 1937 paper written by Keynes for the *Quarterly Journal of Economics* to answer certain criticisms of *The General Theory*, Shackle says that this article 'destroyed in one sentence the basic analysis of conventional economics, that business can and does proceed by reason and calculation based on sufficient data. That basis is absent he said in effect in the nature of things' (Shackle 1974: preface). In a pure barter system, says Shackle, Say's law of markets would hold — that is, supply would create its own demand in a semi-automatic manner and equilibrium, if by chance disturbed, would rapidly re-establish itself. The existence of money increases enormously the possibility that the level of effective demand will be insufficient to guarantee full employment, simply because money absolves those who seek to accumulate wealth out of current production from deciding what real forms this wealth should take, placing the burden of this decision and its consequences on a small number of businessmen. (Important issues about the nature of equilibrium and its place, if any, in the analysis of capitalist economy are raised here. They will be examined later in the work.)

One final matter must be dealt with in this introductory chapter. As we have already noted, for some economists at any rate, Keynes' work marked a fundamental break with the neoclassical economics in the sense that it was concerned with the economy as a whole, and secondly because it rejected the notion of a static equilibrium which stood at the centre of much neoclassical theory. In the resultant attempt to found a new political economy on the basis of Keynes' work, Joan Robinson and others wish to revive certain elements in the classical–Marxian tradition. In what was regarded in the 1960s as a rehabilitation of classical economics, the work of Piero Sraffa has in this regard been of critical significance. [6]

Sraffa has in fact played a seminal part not only in recent controversies surrounding value theory and the criticisms launched at neoclassical economics. In his survey of developments in economic theory during the inter-war period, G.L.S. Shackle (1967), dealing with what he calls the 'age of turmoil', starts his review of the period with the work of Sraffa. He dubs the famous Sraffa article in *The Economic Journal* 'the Sraffa Manifesto of 1926'. This was the contribution in which Sraffa pointed to the fact that the assumption of large-scale production in individual firms (where increasing returns prevail) and the assumption of perfect competition are incompatible. Sraffa's article centres on an examination of the implications of the theory of competition in the light of neoclassical theory, especially in its Marshallian form. By perfect competition, economists refer to that state of affairs where the individual firm is able to sell 'as much as it likes' at a price spontaneously arrived at by the market and independent of the firm's output. But, argued Sraffa, this law stands in a contradictory relationship to the operation of another law which has been at the centre of economic theory from Adam Smith onwards — the law of increasing returns — which asserts that because of the possibility of greater specialisation available to the firm, costs will fall as the size of the firm increases. Thus the following question was posed: if, at each larger output, the firm's unit cost of production is lowered, what is there to prevent the firm's indefinite expansion? And should the firm so expand and swallow up the whole of the market, what is left of the theory of perfect competition?

By attacking the untenability of the notion of perfect competition in the face of the obvious realities of capitalist economy (increasing monopoly, etc.) Sraffa was hitting at what had been seen as one of the centrepieces of nineteenth-century liberal economics, just as Keynes, when he attacked as dogma Say's law of markets, was also proposing to dispose of a law which had been accepted by virtually every orthodox economist for the previous century or so. The fact that in the space of a few years this two-pronged attack should be launched against the most cherished tenets of Manchester economics indicates that a fundamental crisis had been joined for both capitalist economy as well as for one of its ideological expressions, neoclassical economics, which had long taken as a truism the proposition that an unregulated capitalism maximised both the freedom of individual choice as well as the utilisation of existing resources. As is well known, Sraffa proposed that the theory of perfect competition be abandoned in favour of the study of oligopolistic market structures, a lead which Robinson, Edward Chamberlin, and others were to follow in the 1930s. Sraffa's work went in a slightly different, though related direction: to an attempted critique of neoclassical economics which *prima facie* went back to certain themes in classical, especially Ricardian, economics and jettisoned the notion of marginalism (Sraffa 1960).

The Significance of Sraffa

It is on the basis of Sraffa's work that a school of 'neo-Ricardianism' has developed which amongst other things proposes that it is possible to analyse capitalist economy without recourse to the now redundant notions of value and surplus value found in Marx. On the strength of Sraffa's modified version of classical political economy, together with Keynes' notion of effective demand, a new political economy can be established. At least this is the claim.

As we have already indicated, Joan Robinson has been a central figure in all these developments. Standing at the crossroads of various strands in modern economic theory, she is representative of those working for a reconstruction of political economy which will overcome what she and her fellow thinkers see as the bankruptcy of neoclassical economics. Such a political economy would embrace elements from the classical school, as revived in the work of Sraffa, a classical tradition which according to Robinson can be enriched with the contributions of Alfred Marshall, Keynes and Michal Kalecki. From the 1950s onwards she has been attempting

> to trace the confusions and sophistries of current neoclassical doctrine to their origin in the rejection of historic time in the static equilibrium theory of the neoclassical economics and at the same time to find a more hopeful alternative in the classical tradition, revived by Sraffa, which flows from Ricardo through Marx, diluted by Marshall and enriched by the analysis of effective demand of Keynes and Kalecki.

Now there are clearly a series of by no means uncontentious statements here which we shall have to examine in more detail in later chapters. But a number of preliminary points can be made:

1. Robinson speaks of the classical school. But this is far from being an unambiguous theoretical category. Marx invented it, but Keynes used it in a radically different sense in *The General Theory*. As we shall see, this is an important issue which has a fundamental bearing on the nature of Keynes' attempted revolution in economic theory. (When Keynes said he wanted to destroy the Ricardian foundations of Marxism he was in effect conflating their work and especially their theories of value.)

2. The widespread and fashionable use of the appellation neo-Ricardian to characterise the school founded on the basis of Sraffa's work notwithstanding, it is by no means universally accepted, certainly not by Marxists, that his work does in fact represent a return to the classical tradition, at least not as that tradition was understood and criticised by Marx. In the view of the present writer, in essence Sraffa's work involves a degeneration as compared with the high point reached by classical political economy, the work of David Ricardo.

3. A final matter of importance lies in Robinson's assertion that the work of Keynes can be successfully married to that of the classical and/or the Marxist tradition. We shall attempt to demonstrate in Chapter 3 that this is not so and that the standpoint of Keynes was radically different from that of the classical economists and fundamentally different from that of Marx; in this sense the project that Robinson advocates is in the

last resort meaningless and could at best only result in an eclectic mish-mash.

It is of course true that from the 1930s onwards, members of the Cambridge school, with Robinson in the van, made a series of criticisms of aspects of neoclassical orthodox economics, and the 'Keynesian revolution' is best located within the context of this general development. Despite certain differences amongst members of this trend — some would want to draw a distinction between those who owe more to Sraffa than to Keynes, for instance — the substance of this criticism can be said to comprise two points:

1. It attacks the unreality of perfect competition which supposedly ensures, simultaneously, the efficient allocation of resources and consumer sovereignty (leading to the celebrated Pareto optimality).

2. The second issue concerns the question of capital. According to neoclassical theory, the volume of capital is normally determined as capitalised income, depending on the interest on a stock of capital assets (which, in conditions of equilibrium, is identified with the rate of profit). It therefore follows that if the value of capital assets is to be determined, the rate of interest must be known beforehand, but the neoclassical theory claims to explain the size of production-factor incomes, including the rate of interest. The Sraffians thus accuse the neoclassical theory of circularity (see Robinson 1971).

The arguments between the neo-Keynesians and the defenders of classical orthodoxy have certainly been heated, but the question none the less remains: do these two attacks together constitute a fundamental assault on the neoclassical tradition, as is widely believed? Our answer is in the negative, and for the following reasons. Neo-Keynesianism rejects one particular market structure, perfect competition, as no longer corresponding to the reality of modern capitalism. Marx, however, criticised vulgar economy from a quite different angle from that of the Sraffians; Marx rejected entirely the very idea of capital productivity (III: 814–43): living labour alone can create new value, but capital as a value magnitude does not and cannot create such new value: it is merely a condition for its appropriation. For Marx the spurious notion of the 'productivity' of capital arises from the confusion of the value and the physical aspects of capital. That is to say, while capital is a value it is one attached to various and changing things — machinery, raw materials, bank entries, impulses in electronic data banks, etc. And it was precisely this inability on the part of vulgar economy to distinguish critically between qualities of things arising from the social relations of which things were a part, as against the qualities which arose from the material properties of things, that Marx designates as fetishism. The radical Keynesians have made much of the fact that capital, far from being homogeneous, as neoclassical theory proposes, is in point of fact highly heterogeneous. Robinson and her followers have poured scorn on the assumption of orthodox neoclassicism to the effect that capital is like jelly, infinitely malleable; the Cambridge Keynesians wish to stress the fact that capital exists in time and is composed of a wide variety of things — steel, bricks, money, etc. As a survey of their controversies with the neoclassical school puts it:

> Once heterogeneity of capital goods is introduced, the parables based on jelly no longer apply. In particular, it can no longer be argued that 'capital' is paid a marginal product which equals r (even in an equilibrium situation) . . . the finding . . . destroys the foundations of the traditional demand and supply approach to the theory of distribution. (Harcourt 1969: 394)

Now while much has been made of this issue, it really misses the point. The fact is of course that capital, as the post-Keynesians rightly point out, does indeed comprise many changing elements. But the basic matter which has divided economists is not this problem but a far more fundamental one: is capital a 'thing' or is it an expression of a definite social relation of production, albeit one attached to a thing? The Cambridge criticism has nothing of substance to say on this question. (We shall deal more fully with the nature of capital and the confusions surrounding this issue in Chapter 3.)

Just as fundamental a question for the Sraffa wing of the post-Keynesian school is the fact that they singularly fail to criticise the vulgar notion that price is equivalent to value, that the appearance of things is identical with their essence. Indeed, they explicitly reject the law of value as being sheer metaphysics (Joan Robinson), by which they mean that it cannot be empirically tested and, in line with Karl Popper, cannot therefore qualify as having scientific status. In this respect the term neo-Ricardian which has been applied to members of this school is quite inappropriate, for in their rejection of the notion of value and surplus value they take a step backwards from Ricardo, who started from the determination of value by labour time which he sought to make the foundation for his analysis of the inner workings of the capitalist economy. [7] Second, and connected to this point. Unless one accepts the determination of value by labour time one cannot logically demonstrate that the relations of distribution arise out of production relations. We shall not be concerned in this book with the distribution theories of the left-Keynesians such as

Robinson, Kaldor, etc., but in general they rest upon the proposition that the distribution of wealth is determined by the operations of savings and investment outside the actual process of production. (Here the Cambridge school relies heavily on the work of Michal Kalecki.)

In this chapter we have aimed to sketch out the historical and theoretical background to the current crisis of Keynesian economics. It remains to outline the contents of each of the chapters which follows.

In Chapter 2 we shall assess the nature and significance of the Keynesian revolution from the point of view of its implications for economic policy as well as in the light of the fundamental change Keynes claimed to have made in the field of economic theory. If not amongst all academic economists, then certainly amongst the educated public it was believed that it was above all thanks to the success of the Keynesian revolution that capitalism enjoyed an unprecedented degree of success after 1945. This view is, to put it mildly, open to serious question. It will be suggested that the post-war boom had nothing centrally to do with the application of Keynesian policies and further, against the claims of many economists and economic historians, Keynesianism, it will be argued, offered no real solutions to the crisis of the 1930s. In short it will be proposed that the increasing intervention of the state in the post-war economy owed little, if anything, to a conversion to Keynesian ideas but was a reflection of the economic/political and social problems of capitalism at a definite historical point. Further, it will be suggested that the trend towards a growing intervention by the state in a wide range of economic and social matters is a development organic to the very nature of twentieth-century capitalism in all countries, is not fundamentally an ideological matter and as such was in no way inspired by Keynesian economic theory. Having said this, there is no doubt that, within the Anglo-Saxon world at least, Keynes' name is the main one associated with the idea of growing state involvement in the economy. Keynes' views of this question will be considered in the light of the history of economic thought in both Britain and more generally in Europe. As already noted, Keynesianism became the fundamental element in post-war social democratic ideology. But it will be argued that there is nothing necessarily liberal or progressive about Keynesian proposals and that they can be and indeed have been the vehicle for a variety of social and intellectual purposes.

This will lead (Chapter 3) to a detailed analysis of the theoretical foundations of Keynes' *General Theory*. The basic categories of this work will be subject to critical scrutiny and it will be argued that they are of an essentially subjective character which not only renders them incapable of explaining the dynamics of bourgeois economy but also opens up the possibility that they could be filled with any social and political content, a fact which explains the wide use to which Keynesian ideas have in fact been put. Specific attention will be given to the concept of capital held by Keynes as well as by his most influential followers such as Robinson, on the grounds that this is the fundamental category of bourgeois economy and the treatment of it by any particular writer is in this sense a litmus test as to their position on every crucial economic question. Because Keynes has often been presented as above all an opponent of equilibrium economics, the notion of equilibrium and its place in an analysis of capitalist economy will be critically reviewed. It will be argued that the angle from which Marx and Keynes began their analyses of the capitalist economy were of a wholly different nature and it will be maintained that Keynes belongs not to the classical tradition in economics but to the vulgar school. It will be strongly argued that it is not possible to construct bridges between the political economy of Marx and that of Keynes, as envisaged by Robinson and others.

Chapter 4 will deal more directly with the nature of the post-war inflationary boom and its unfolding contradictions. Attention here will be given to the nature of state spending as it was understood by Keynesianism and the inadequacy of such understanding will be considered. The forces generating the increased state spending of the post-war period will be examined and it will be suggested that it arose not merely from a series of narrowly conceived 'economic' needs which capitalism experienced but also from a number of social and political pressures which in the concrete conditions emerging after the last world war capitalism found unable to resist. It is in this light that the thesis to the effect that a too large volume of state spending is the root cause of capitalism's crisis (Bacon, Eltis *et al.*) will be considered: here it will be proposed that such state expenditure cannot be construed as the source of the crisis but rather as one of its principal effects. This chapter will seek to show that the claims of the Sraffa school notwithstanding, it is not possible to understand the developing contradictions of the post-war boom without recourse to the basic categories and laws of Marxist political economy, especially the law of value and the law of the tendency of the rate of profit to fall.

At the end of his life Keynes was centrally concerned with proposals for reshaping the nature of the international economy. The post-war economy developed within the framework of an international economic order which Keynes himself had helped to shape. Chapter 5 will therefore deal with the nature of the Bretton Woods arrangements and the seeds of their effective disintegration in the 1970s when the US removed gold backing for the dollar, the single event which more than any other unleashed severe inflationary pressures and threw Keynesianism into a fundamental crisis. This will enable us to locate the crisis of Keynesianism within its international context.

Finally, the several topics of the work will be drawn together, the continued central relevance of Marxism stressed, and some suggestions for further work on the themes dealt with in the book suggested. In particular those attempts to provide an alternative to the doctrines of monetarism on the basis of Keynesianism and along the lines of the Alternative Economic Strategy will be subjected to critical scrutiny, and it will be argued that there can be no prospect of a revival for Keynesian economics, for the good reason that this trend in economic theory and policy emerged as a dominant ideological force only under definite historical economic and political circumstances; circumstances which have now disappeared.

Notes

1. Referring to the phenomenon which became fashionably know as stagflation, Lord Kaldor said, 'Nothing of this kind has ever occurred before in peace time — I mean an inflation of that magnitude encompassing not just one or two countries, but all the leading industrial countries of the world. The other unique feature of this inflation was that it was accompanied by a marked recession in industrial production. . . . This combination of inflation and industrial recession is a new phenomenon, the explanation of which presents an intellectual challenge to economists' (Kaldor 1978: 215). Other economists took an even more sombre view of the implications of world-wide inflation. Thus at the end of the 1970s two prominent economists could say, 'In the past decade, the problem of inflation has escalated from a continuing irritant to a blight on the stability and efficient performance of the leading economies and to a potential threat to the preservation of democratic societies' (Hirsch and Goldthorpe 1978: 1). One of the casualties of the explosion of inflation in the 1970s, occurring alongside rising unemployment, was the much vaunted Phillips curve which had postulated a trade-off between inflation and unemployment.

2. The subjectivity of such views is clear: they seek to explain fundamental crises in the system as the result of incorrect financial policies pursued by governments. Here monetarism attempts to explain capitalist crises as originating in the sphere of circulation rather than in the process of production. Further, for the monetarists, such crises are not economic but political, stemming as they do from unwise state policies. As with bourgeois economics as a whole, when the moment comes to explain an economic crisis, economic factors are abandoned in favour of non-economic phenomena.

3. Without anticipating too much of the later discussion it can be noted that amongst the notions of the vulgar economists Marx considered one of the most vulgar, that which explained rising prices by resort to increases in the supply of money. 'The idea that the banks had unduly expanded the currency, thus producing an inflation of prices violently to be readjusted by a final collapse, is too cheap a method for accounting for every crisis not to be eagerly caught at. . . . The vulgar notion, therefore, which refers the recent crisis and crises generally to an over-issue of bank notes, must be discarded as altogether imaginary' (MECW 16: 8).

4. In connection with the often acrimonious dispute between the monetarists and the Keynesians, one can truly say that, as far as economics is concerned, there is little new under the sun. For this controversy is essentially a re-run of the nineteenth-century one

between those such as Ricardo defending the 'currency principle' and Tooke and others who adhered to the 'banking principle'. The former school held that the price level depended on the amount of money in circulation and that, internationally, prices expressed the purchasing power of each national currency. Equilibrium between national economies was established by the transfer of coin and bullion. Excess of Bank of England notes was the cause of inflation and such notes should therefore be kept to the level of gold deposits in the Bank of England. Opposing this view, the banking school claimed that price movements rested on public confidence in the currency. The quantity of money in circulation depended on public demand, the quantity of bank notes being an effect and not a cause of the demand for them. In other words the Bank simply issued what was required of it. As Marx noted, 'But continued investigation of the history of prices compelled Tooke to recognise . . . that increases or decreases in the amount of currency when the value of the precious metals remains constant are always the consequence, never the cause of price variations, that altogether the circulation of money is merely a secondary movement' (Marx 1971: 186).

5. In another place, Balogh declares: 'The Keynesian revolution in economic thought has proved as broken a reed in helping to attain a steady dynamism in our economy as the elegant structure of thought it overcame. . . . Liberal Keynesian growthmanship did achieve accelerated and sustained growth. But through the social tensions, which were caused by its failure to secure a sense of justice, it undermined its own success through escalating demands for higher money incomes' (Balogh 1971).

6. In a perceptive review, Hutchison noted the change in Dobb's position on the nature of the 'marginalist revolution'. In his early work, Dobb had attached little significance to this event, seeing it as an extension of elements already present in the vulgar economy which emerged to a position of dominance from the 1830s onwards. In his later work he saw it as a decisive turning-point, and constituting a far more decisive revolution than that for which Keynes was responsible in the 1930s. This 'conversion' Hutchison explains in terms of Dobb's aim to highlight the supposed revolutionary character of Sraffa's work; he is building up what Sraffa (according to Dobb) has overthrown (Hutchison: 1978). Dobb claims that Sraffa (along with Robinson and other critics) are heirs to the Ricardian–Marxist tradition in analysing the problems of exchange and distribution (Dobb 1973: 111). Ronald Meek (1964) takes a similar position to Dobb. Amongst other things both tend to identify Ricardian political economy with Marx's critique of it.

7. A good examination of the gulf dividing Sraffa from the classical tradition (let alone from the position of Marx) is provided by S. Himmelweit and S. Mohun, in Steedman *et al.* (1981).

2 THE SIGNIFICANCE OF THE KEYNESIAN REVOLUTION

. . . the ideas of economists and political philosophers, both when they are right and when they are wrong, are more powerful than is commonly understood. Indeed the world is ruled by little else. Practical men, who believe themselves to be quite exempt from intellectual influences, are usually the slave of some defunct economist. Madmen in authority, who hear voices in the air, are distilling their frenzy from some academic scribbler of a few years back. I am sure that the power of vested interests is vastly exaggerated compared with the gradual encroachment of ideas . . . sooner or later, it is ideas, not vested interests, which are dangerous for good or evil. (GT: 383–4)

I believe myself to be writing a book on economic theory whch will largely revolutionise . . . the way the world thinks about economic problems. When my new theory has been duly assimilated and mixed with politics and feelings and passions, I can't predict what the final upshot will be in its effect on actions and affairs. But there will be a great change, and in particular the Ricardian foundations of Marxism will be knocked away. (Keynes to George Bernard Shaw, 1 January 1935)

The conventional view about the Keynesian revolution and its implications for economic policy held, until recently at least, by most economists ran something like this. An entrenched orthodoxy ('the Treasury view' or 'sound finance') dominated the formulation of economic policy until the outbreak of the Second World War. Only then did Keynes' revolution triumph when it won over a tier of influential politicians and those in the upper echelons of the state bureaucracy. Thanks to their conversion to Keynes' teachings, economic policy took a new turn, with post-war governments committed to full employment and for the first time in possession of the tools to meet that commitment. And as a result of these policies, full employment was secured for more than three decades. Only recently, for reasons which are not immediately clear, have Keynesian policies been dropped, producing once again conditions of high unemployment and industrial slump. This scenario, we shall argue, is highly questionable on at least three important counts:

1. It accepts Keynes' own belief in the primacy of ideas in the shaping

of state economic policy. An examination of the development of the role of the state indicates that there is an organic trend towards ever greater state involvement in the attempted regulation of economic and social matters and Keynesianism was merely one, but only one, expression of this tendency which took specific forms in the case of Britain during and after the Second World War.

2. It takes *prima facie* the proposition that Keynesianism was actually put into operation after 1945; Keynesianism here being taken to mean the manipulation of the state budget in order to secure a level of effective demand sufficient to generate full employment. As many have now pointed out, this is a highly dubious contention, certainly as far as British economic policy is concerned.

3. It concurs with Keynes' own judgement about the significance of his work: namely that it did in fact constitute a revolution in economics. We have already noted that there is little if any agreement amongst those who would wish to be labelled Keynesians about the nature of this revolution. Some see it as an adaptation of the old liberal economics, some as a decisively new way of conceiving economic problems. In looking at each of these questions in some detail we shall be concerned with a series of interrelated matters.

1. We shall explore the nature of state intervention in the economy as this is understood by Marxism. Then we shall examine the reflection of the tendency towards the acceptance of state intervention in English economic thought prior to Keynes. We shall discover that the tenets of the old liberal neoclassical economics, and the corollary of these tenets, *laissez-faire* as an economic doctrine, were under considerable challenge before *The General Theory* appeared and that in this respect Keynes was giving expression, albeit a somewhat extreme one, to a definite trend in economic thought. We shall also examine the extent to which the neoclassical economists whom Keynes attacked with such relish in *The General Theory* did actually carry their theory into practice when it came to the big question which they faced in the 1930s, namely unemployment.

2. The greater involvement of the state in twentieth-century capitalism is an international phenomenon which was actually taken much further in other countries than in Britain, traditional home of free trade and the doctrine of the minimal state. There is no doubt that state regulation reached its zenith in the case of Fascist theory and practice, and we shall therefore examine Keynesian doctrine in the light of this fact.

3. There is now widespread doubt about the operation of Keynesian policies in Britain after 1945. The inflationary boom, it is suggested, had little if anything to do with the conscious application of Keynesian policies.

We shall review critically the recent controversies on this question but also extend the discussion to include two further matters. Many have argued that Keynesianism was quite unsuited for the purposes to which it was put in the post-war period — as an instrument for securing economic growth or for fine tuning the economy; it was, however, an economic theory designed for and suited to attacking the problem which dominated the period in which it was born — the problem was mass unemployment. We shall therefore examine the extent to which, had it been applied in the 1930s, it could have hoped to have solved this problem.

4. The nature of Keynes' criticisms of neoclassical theory will be examined in the light of the history of economic thought. As is well known, Keynes drew upon the work of a number of previous thinkers, some well known, such as Malthus, others less so, such as Gessel and Major Douglas. (That he did so in such an eclectic manner is perhaps one reason why there is little agreement about the substance of the 'real Keynes'.) An examination of this earlier work will allow a judgement about the nature of the Keynesian revolution and the relationship of its initiator to previous trends in economic thought.

5. Marxism, historical materialism, insists that ideas are, in the final analysis, a reflection of the social relations of production. Keynes was not critical of the capitalist economic system as such, but he did call into question certain features of the system as they presented themselves in the twentieth century. In the course of this chapter we shall examine Keynes' objections to certain features of capitalism and assess their historical significance.

Marxism on the Increasing Role of the State

For Marxism the inexorable tendency towards state intervention in the functioning and attempted regulation of the capitalist economy has as little to do with abstractly arrived at policy options as has the onset of war in the present century. Here its view differs radically from that of Keynes and the Keynesians generally. Thus while it can be argued that of all those attempting to explain and justify (often, it must be said, to a sceptical audience) the necessity for greater state involvement in economic and social matters Keynes occupies the most important position, at least as far as the Anglo-Saxon world goes, it would be quite wrong to believe that such state intervention actually flowed from the theoretical work of Keynes and others. To take such a stance would be to confuse cause with effect. In general it can be said that it was the sharpening contradictions engendered by the growth of the productive forces, and in particular the accelerating trend towards monopoly (reaching a nodal point with the onset of the twentieth century) which provide the real material foundation making inescapable a greatly increased activity on the state's part. The emergence of joint stock companies in the period after 1870, said Marx, 'establishes a monopoly in certain spheres and thereby requires state interference' (III: 438), a point reiterated by Engels in *Socialism Utopian and Scientific* when he says, 'In any case, with trusts or without, the official representatives of capitalist society — the state — will ultimately have to undertake the direction of production' (Marx and Engels 1977 vol. 3: 144).

Here we provide only the briefest sketch of the general conception which Marxism holds about the nature of state intervention in capitalist economy. It is necessary to make two broad points. First, and without entering into the considerable recent controversy on this issue, Marxism rejects unambiguously the notion (one which is implicit in Keynes) to the effect that the state is a neutral instrument, standing above classes, an arbitrator representing the 'general will', or whatever. Marxism understands the state as arising only with the appearance of classes in history and thus views it as an instrument of class rule. The nature of the state's operations, within the sphere of the economy and without, and the limits to that operation are in the last resort determined by this decisive fact, one quite independent of the particular form taken by the capitalist state (whether parliamentary democracy, military dictatorship, etc.). Second — and this once more has been the subject of a considerable literature which cannot be dealt with here — it is a travesty of Marxism to suggest that the state is a mere reflex of economic conditions, only a mechanical reflection of the social relations of production. The state, even though it arises on definite historically formed economic conditions, is an active element always, one of the forces helping shape those economic conditions. Thus Lenin: 'The state can on no account be something inert, it always acts and acts very energetically, it is always active and never passive' (LCW 1: 355). And this same point was made earlier by Engels in some of his last letters when he attempted to overcome a tendency towards mechanical materialism amongst certain Marxists at the time. Writing to Conrad Schmidt he points out that under capitalism there exists an

> interaction of two unequal forces: on the one hand, the economic movement, on the other hand, the new political power, which strives for as much independence as possible and which, having once been

established is endowed with relative independence. (Marx and Engels 1956: 421)

In looking at the nature of the growing intrusion of the state into economic matters it will be convenient to outline the way in which Engels presents the question in his *Anti-Dühring*. In listing the developing contradictions of capitalist economy, Engels sees them all as reflections of what is in the last resort the fundamental contradiction of this mode of production: an historical tendency for the productive forces to come into ever sharper conflict with the existing property relations. Thus Engels outlines the following points: First, the ever growing tendency towards the socialisation of production under capitalism. Production is never carried out by individuals; Adam Smith's Robinson Crusoe is an historical myth precisely because production is always a social process involving, amongst other things, a division of labour, and this fact is true of all social systems but more than ever true of capitalism. Under capitalism this growing socialisation takes a number of forms, chief amongst them being in the first place an ever more intricate division of labour, not merely within enterprises (for Adam Smith the main point) nor between enterprises only but between whole branches of the economy. Second, the growth in the scale of production which brings with it the emergence of monopoly as a dominant economic form from the end of the nineteenth century onwards. Both of these trends — the increasingly socialised character of production and the development towards monopoly — make imperative a growing degree of state interference, principally designed to regulate relations between branches of an economy which exhibits a growing tendency towards an unevenness of development.

One consequence of the increasing scale of operation within capitalist economy is the fact that the capital necessary for production tends in many branches to be beyond the reach of even the largest capitals and only the state is able to mobilise resources on the scale required. Thus says Marx:

Any country, for instance the United States, might feel the need in production relations for railways, in spite of this, the benefit . . . derived by production from the existence of railways might be so negligible that the advance of capital for this purpose would be nothing but a loss of money. Then capital transfers these outlays onto the shoulders of the state. (Quoted in Pevsner 1982: 15)

And further:

[capital] always strives only to achieve particular conditions for increasing its value, while the conditions that are common for everything it foists onto the whole community as national requirements. Capital only undertakes operations that are profitable from its own point of view. (ibid.)

Engels points to a related contradiction: that between the growth of 'planning' within the individual enterprise on the one hand (a feature which in contemporary capitalism takes the form of the use of operations research, cybernetics, etc.), and the growing anarchy prevalent between such highly organised enterprises. (The term 'anarchy' is employed here in its literal sense to mean the absence of any *a priori* regulation, the lack of any purposeful plan.) Here again the state was driven to abandon the precepts of *laissez-faire* in order that it might try to deal with the resultant problems.

Finally, Engels draws attention to one decisive contradiction which the development of capitalism entails: that between the world economy and a world division of labour on the one hand, and the existence of the nation state on the other. Here again the state is obliged to assume the role of the defender of the national capital and the instrument through which such capital seeks to secure its economic, commercial, military etc. interests, in competition with its rivals.

One potent factor driving towards state intervention, even in the period prior to that designated by Marxists as the imperialist epoch, is the fact that the increasing socialisation of production brings with it not a lessening of the contradictions between various capitals (as revisionism from the time of Bernstein onwards proclaimed to be the case) but on the very contrary their rapid sharpening. As far as the present century is concerned these contradictions reach the peak of development in war when tendencies inherent in a previously peaceful phase manifest themselves. It is thus inevitable that the functions of the state — price-fixing, direction of labour, military conscription, etc. — should be raised to new heights in such periods.

Keynes: Laissez-Faire and the Role of the State

Whatever conclusions are arrived at concerning the questions raised at the start of this chapter and the others which they entail, it is undoubtedly true that Keynes has to be considered one of the central forces of modern (that is, twentieth-century) theories of the state regulation of the capitalist economy. Whatever the quality of his conceptions, there can be no doubting the ideological import of this aspect of his work. For it is on the basis of the growing role of the state that theories about the alleged transformation of post-war capitalism were mainly if not exclusively founded. (There were several theories in the 1930s about the negation of capitalism which was then supposedly taking place, amongst them being James Burnham's thesis concerning the managerial revolution, but they owed little if anything to the ideas of Keynes.) In this respect, because he gave a central place to the state in the functioning of the economy, Keynes may truly be looked upon as one of the initiators of the dominant trend in the political economics of the present century.

The principal complaint Keynes lodged against the old (neoclassical) economics was that he saw its basic assumptions as being increasingly out of line with the new conditions emerging in the present century. At one point in *The General Theory*, commenting on this increasing lack of correspondence between the old neoclassical theory and the observed developments of the capitalist system, Keynes says:

> For professional economists, after Malthus, were apparently unmoved by the lack of correspondence between the results of their theory and the facts of observation. . . . It may well be that the classical theory represents the way in which we should like our Economy to behave. But to assume that it actually does so is to assume our difficulties away. (GT)

Here Keynes is pursuing his well-known theme: that the only measure that could be employed to pass judgement on what he termed classical economics was the question of whether it was capable of serving as a theoretical support to solve the immediate problems of the real world. He is not, we repeat, primarily concerned with the logical deficiencies of neoclassical economics but with the irrelevance of its basic postulates. And because he found those postulates increasingly at odds with reality it could not be concluded that there was an automatic coincidence of the striving by the individual for maximum gain and the social good. Thus 'The world is not so governed from above that private and social interests always co-incide. . . . It is not a correct deduction from the Principles of Economics that enlightened self-interest always operates in the public interest' (JMK CW 9).

Despite the many efforts to present Keynes as some sort of radical opponent of capitalism, it must be emphasised at the outset that whatever partial objections he may have held about what he called the classical economic tradition, and whatever his particular criticisms of the capitalism extant in his lifetime, Keynes none the less remained a staunch defender of the capitalist order. Thus in *The End of Laissez-Faire* he hopes that 'capitalism wisely managed, can probably be made more efficient for attaining economic ends than any alternative system yet in sight.' Here the key words are, of course, 'wisely managed'. Keynes believed in 'the transition from economic anarchy to a regime which deliberately aims at controlling and directing economic forces in the interests of social justice and social stability'.

The nub of his objection to the 'old' unregulated capitalism lay in the fact that he feared it was quite unable in practice to attain this social stability. It was this anxiety which led him to a pragmatic–utilitarian justification of *ad hoc* state intervention. This is a position by no means unique to Keynes. It was one which, broadly speaking, had been advocated from the 1880s onwards by the Fabians for instance who, incidentally, like Keynes believed in a society run by a mandarin élite. Thus in *Fabian Essays*, first published in 1889, we find Sydney Webb, Shaw and co. proposing in a manner strikingly prefiguring Keynes that receivers of rent and interest are to be gradually abolished — in their case by means of a progressive taxation. In his contribution to the *Essays* William Clarke drew attention to the rapid advance of monopoly and with it the separation of the functions of management from ownership (a favourite theme for post-1945 social democratic theorists). He went on,

> the capitalist is fast becoming absolutely useless. Finding it easier and more rational to combine with others of his class in a large undertaking, he has now abdicated his position of overseer, has put in a salaried manager to perform his work for him, and has become a mere rent or interest receiver. The rent or interest he receives is paid for the use of a monopoly which not he but a whole multitude of people created by their joint efforts. (Briggs 1962: 117)

Behind Fabian thinking was the idea that the end of *laissez-faire* was tantamount to the end of capitalism, at least a capitalism prone to crisis and breakdown. It is always possible to take one relative form of capitalism — in this case *laissez-faire* capitalism — and suggest that in some way it is the essential form, but one which is now passing away, if indeed it has not already disappeared. Sir Karl Popper, for instance, declared that 'what Marx called "capitalism" i.e. *laissez-faire* capitalism, has completely "withered away" in the twentieth century' (Popper 1947, vol. 2: 318). In other words, Popper, quite illegitimately, takes one passing form of capital, its competitive phase, and raises it to the rank of essential form. Naturally any historical judgement on capital, the relationship between its various forms and the necessity for the passage of one into the other, is avoided by this sort of metaphysical approach. It is just this historical conception of capitalism which is absent in Keynes.[1] His disavowal of *laissez-faire* is a pragmatic–utilitarian one. It is the only way to save the system. Thus in *The General Theory* he says:

> Whilst, therefore, the enlargement of the functions of government, in-
> volved in the task of adjusting to one another the propensity to con-
> sume and the inducement to invest, would seem to a nineteenth-century
> publicist or a contemporary American financier to be a terrific en-
> croachment on individualism, I defend it, on the contrary, both as the
> only practicable means of avoiding the destruction of existing economic
> forms in their entirety and as the condition of the successful function-
> ing of individual initiative. (GT: 380)

In short, further state intervention was necessary to rescue the capitalist system, a point reiterated in different form when Keynes says 'Our final task might be to select those variables which can be deliberately con-trolled or managed by central authority in the kind of system in which we actually live' (GT: 247). Rendered into concrete terms this meant that any variables might be selected within the economic system: the choice of the appropriate ones would be judged from the point of view of their effectiveness and applicability in preserving existing economic forms. Naturally disputes could, and in point of fact did, arise about the efficacy of the control of any one particular variable. The monetarists would point to the crucial role played by the regulation of the money supply, the or-thodox Keynesians to the control of government spending and the level of investment. Despite the great heat generated amongst the participants in these controversies they are in reality of relatively minor significance.[2] But in any event, for Keynes such operations by the state (his 'central authority') would be based on one crucial condition: that the foundations of capitalist economy ('the kind of system in which we actually live') would be preserved intact.

According to neoclassical theory, the economy is regulated by the market, through which the consumer makes his demands on it; accor-ding to this conception the state does not deal with the consumer but only with the will of the citizens (the electors) who, through the market, make their needs felt in connection with the fulfilling of social re-quirements. For this purpose a share of income is set aside in the form of taxes. In contrast to this theory, Keynes held that the state's responsibility was considerably more extensive, for he believed that not only must it regulate the economy in order to ensure full employment, but it would be obliged to carry through measures to generate sufficient investments to compensate for what he considered to be a chronic shortfall of private investments. In the view of Keynes, the state should employ the national income, or at any rate a proportion of it, in order to alleviate unemployment, a fact which made the state a central component of the economic system rather than an external force, as it had on the whole been in the case of the old neoclassical concept. It was principally on the strength of this aspect of Keynes' theory that apologists for capitalism were at a later stage (after 1945) to propose that the spontaneous operation of the market system — which it was widely accepted had broken down irrevocably in the 1930s — was yielding to state regulation, or statism, as it was widely known. It was from this idea that the notion of 'welfare capitalism' was derived, with its view of the state as a supra-class force looking after all members of society regardless of their social position. This in turn provided the justification for the policies of those who dominated social democracy in Britain after 1945, and we shall have more to say of this issue presently.

As is well known, Keynes combined his belief that capitalism suffered from an inadequate number of outlets for profitable investment with proposals for a modest degree of income redistribution as one way in which effective demand might be raised. These prescriptions were in turn derived from Keynes' view of consumption: a more equitable distribution of income was one way of raising consumption. Here again, in advocating state measures to regulate the distribution of income, Keynes found himself at odds with the old neoclassical tradition where such things were supposedly arrived at spontaneously by the play of market forces.

Another aspect worthy of note is Keynes' view about the determination of wages. It is widely held that Keynes was opposed to certain aspects of the wages theory to which neoclassical economics subscribed. But in this case, as in many others, the differences with his predecessors were ones of a secondary rather than a substantive character. As recent writers (Meltzer 1981; Hutchison 1981) have noted, Keynes never challenged fundamentally the marginal productivity theory of wages, nor therefore in the last resort did he deny that a reduction in wages was the *quid pro quo* for an increase in the level of employment. What he did argue was that the seeming geometric decline in employment which capitalism experienced as *The General Theory* was being prepared was due not so much to microeconomic as to macroeconomic factors, notably a shortage of investment and a deficiency of aggregate demand. (This point would of course be disputed by the monetarists: for them, once a sound money policy is instituted, the functioning of the economy depends essentially upon microeconomic factors.) This apart, Keynes believed that direct wage cuts were socially dangerous, for they would almost inevitably meet with fierce resistance on the part of the working class. Keynes proposed that wages be reduced covertly, through the medium of a state-regulated process of inflation: 'A movement by employers to revise money-wage bargains downward will be much more strongly resisted than a gradual and automatic lowering of real wages as a result of rising prices' (GT: 264). Such a controlled inflation would allow for an increase in nominal wages while affecting a simultaneous reduction in real wages through a price inflation, which would also help to boost profits. Thus on the question of the level of wages and their determination, Keynes placed the state at the centre of his concerns. At one point in *The General Theory* he says:

> It is not the ownership of the instruments of production which it is important for the State to assume. If the State is able to determine the aggregate amount of resources devoted to augmenting the instruments and the basic rate of reward to those who own them, it will have accomplished all that it is necessary. (GT: 378)

Keynes here proposes that the state be responsible for the determination of the rate of reward to capital which, by implication, is no longer to be left for market forces to determine. It was from his lead that arguments for state-controlled 'incomes policies' were taken, arguments which have been advocated principally by the post-Keynesians and justified as the best instrument for ensuring price stability. (The theoretical issue is as follows: according to the post-Keynesians, one result of the misreading of Keynes has been the wrong diagnosis of inflation. During the post-war years inflation had been understood as being caused by excess demand rather than as a consequence of the pressure on costs. As a result the response by governments to inflationary pressures was invariably to cut demand which, while it certainly reduced output and thereby raised unemployment, made little or no impact on prices.)

Keynes' ideas are by no means of purely academic interest, for they have quite profound political implications, not least for the nature and role of trade unionism within the capitalist system. One of the principal features of nineteenth-century British capitalism in its liberal phase of development was the granting of certain concessions to the organised trade union movement which was allowed to bargain collectively with employers on questions of wages and working conditions. The present century has brought a steady movement away from such arrangements, a development which has speeded up in the last two decades. All British governments, whether Conservative or Labour, have tended towards some form of corporatism, in which the rights of the unions as independent bargainers on behalf of their members have been eroded. Here this aspect of Keynes' work was entirely consonant with some of the basic social and political trends of the century.

It should be noted that although Keynes did undoubtedly rely upon the theoretical work of certain of his predecessors, albeit in a highly eclectic manner, his views were also founded upon a considerable practical experience, stretching from his proposals for the reform of the Indian currency system to his work at the end of his life for a new world monetary order. Keynes was an adviser to the government in the First World War, through the period of the Versailles Treaty negotiations as well as during the subsequent attempted restoration and final abandonment of the old Gold Standard in 1931. Although we leave aside until the next chapter a detailed consideration of the nature of Keynes' theoretical innovations, it can provisionally be asserted that it was largely on the basis of this practical and theoretical work, culminating in *The General Theory*, that the path was prepared for the notion that the twentieth century marked the nemesis of the age of free competition; for the idea that the economy was no longer able to function and regulate itself without the intervention of a third force (the state) to restore the now inherent imbalance of production (represented by Keynes as a flow of incomes) and consumption.

Nor were Keynes' ideas merely an immediate response to the slump which engulfed the capitalist world in the period after 1929. His views on economic policy and economic theory alike had deeper roots: they were the outcome of reflections on the problems of economic management under the new conditions of the twentieth century which stretch back until at least the end of the First World War. In his *The End of Laissez-Faire*, given first as a lecture in Oxford in 1924, Keynes says:

> We must aim at separating those services which are technically social from those which are technically individual. The most important items on the Agenda of the State relate not to those activities which private individuals are already fulfilling, but to those activities which fall outside the sphere of the individual, to those decisions which are made by no one if the State does not make them. The important thing for

Government is not to do things which individuals are doing already, and to do them a little better or a little worse, but to do those things which at present are not done at all. (JMK CW 9)

Thus was the imperative of state intervention justified.

Here Keynes is expressing the fact that his life spanned that period which witnessed the break-up of the old liberalism: the ideology which had justified British social and economic policy to the rest of the world throughout much of the nineteenth century. The beginning of Britain's secular decline, which had its roots in the last decades of the nineteenth century, was the phenomenon undoubtedly dominating Keynes' thought and action throughout his life. In the political sphere it was a loss of world hegemony which found expression in the decline and eventual disintegration of the Liberal Party as the principal political instrument of the ruling class in favour of the Conservative Party. In the field of economics it was a decline which brought about an increasing challenge to and eventual demise of the old 'Manchester economics' which proclaimed free trade and economic liberalism as the twin virtues which would guide Britain and the world to uninterrupted prosperity and peace. (Not that the rest of the world necessarily subscribed to these propositions!) By the 1930s both these props of nineteenth-century bourgeois ideology were under frontal attack, and from many standpoints. The doctrine of *laissez-faire* was being replaced by various notions of 'statism', the most intense expression of this trend coming in Germany, a country where Manchester economics had never in any case cut much ice. That free competition had broken down in favour of monopoly, and this being so the state had to assume responsibility for the regulation of the monopolies, was one of the central motifs of Fascist economic 'theory'.[3] Precisely because Keynes was no academic recluse but was throughout his life intimately concerned with the economic and social problems of twentieth-century capitalism, he was obliged to deal with these central matters of economic theory and policy. Keynes held that overproduction arises from what he regarded as an inherent psychological law, to the effect that as incomes rise so also does consumption, but not as rapidly. As a result, the increase in incomes is accompanied by a greater tendency to save. Investment however fails to increase with sufficient speed to match this rising volume of savings so an unused residual is created, manifesting itself in a less than full use of resources, both human and material. The Victorian view that thrift was amongst the greatest of virtues was no longer appropriate for the twentieth century; indeed, too great a level of savings was one of the causes of our present malaise, said Keynes. He took this discrepancy between saving and investment to be so chronic that its elimination was impossible without systematic state intervention, including a government policy of low interest rates, together with the creation of money and credit in excess of the requirements of immediate circulation, with the concentration in the hands of the state of a part of total income and investment. (Keynes spoke somewhat vaguely about the 'socialisation of investment', and it was from such statements that the idea was quite falsely derived that he was somehow an advocate of socialism, an ill-founded view widespread in American big business circles after 1945.)

Keynes' theory has usually been regarded as an underinvestment theory, in that he saw the problem of capitalism as essentially one associated with the deficiency of investment expenditure. At the same time, however, Keynes was a great admirer of the underconsumptionist Malthus, bitterly regretting the fact that Ricardo's ideas, rather than those of Malthus, had triumphed in the history of English economic thought. And in one respect there are certainly striking similarities in the work of Malthus and Keynes, not least in the fact that both saw the need for a 'third person' outside the relations of capital as a means of correcting the tendency towards unemployment; in the former case such a 'third person' comprised the various non-productive classes; in the case of Keynes the role was to be filled by the state. Others with similar views included Sismondi who saw the petty bourgeois as a necessary third person and the radical economist J.A. Hobson who believed that the colonies provided an outlet for surplus goods generated by capitalism. [4]

Now, in their own particular way, each of these writers was a 'critic' of the capitalist system — but the criticism was in each case of a severely limited character. Even in the case of Hobson, whose social and political views were markedly to the left of Keynes', he believed that the contradictions of capitalism could be surmounted through a radical redistribution of income. The point here is as follows. A mere recognition by a particular writer of certain contradictions associated with capitalism does not thereby necessarily render that work scientific, and Malthus is a case which testifies to the truth of that proposition. For while Malthus did see a certain contradiction between production and consumption, he never probed to the real inner source of this contradiction and Marx was able to declare his work both vulgar (concerned merely with the appearance of the contradictions of the capitalist system but not their essence) and thoroughly apologetic (Malthus 'that shameless sycophant', 'that Parson'). [5] John Stuart Mill is another example of a thinker who opposed certain of capitalism's features and made a series of proposals to rectify these 'faults', including, in his case, a call for a somewhat more equitable distribution of income and a limited extension of the state's functions. And so with Keynes: he accepted that certain problems were associated with capitalism (a denial of such a palpable fact was in any case virtually impossible in the conditions under which *The General Theory* was written) but in effect assumed that, in essence, capital was harmonious. The disharmonious world of appearances arises from factors which contradict this notion and cannot be explained on its basis; in short, they stem from forces outside the economic system — 'wrong policies'; the obduracy or stupidity of those in power; the harmful effect of monopoly, and so on. Hence, in the final resort, Keynes, as do the monetarists, is obliged to explain the collapse of capitalism in the 1930s by means of non-economic factors.

Keynes directed much of his criticisms of the existing economic and social order not against capitalism as such but against one of its forms, namely interest-bearing capital. Thus in a well-known passage he says:

> I see, therefore, the *rentier* aspect of capitalism as a transitional phase which will disappear when it has done its work. And with the disappearance of this *rentier* aspect much else within it will suffer a sea-change. It will be, moreover, a great advantage of the order of events which I am advocating, that the euthanasia of the *rentier*, of the functionless investor, will be nothing sudden, merely a gradual but prolonged continuance of what we have seen recently in Great Britain, and will need no revolution. (GT: 376)

This opposition to the *rentier* was clearly one of the reasons why Keynes opposed the deflationary policies pursued in the 1920s, for deflation 'involves a transference of wealth from the rest of the community to the rentier class . . . from the active to the inactive' (JMK CW 4).

Keynes was certainly not original in taking this stance: others before him had adopted a similar position, just as some of his contemporaries also denounced non-industrial capital, often in far more strident terms. Proudhon was a case of an earlier thinker who attacked the function of the *rentier*: according to Proudhon it is the entrepreneur who stimulates production and if enterprise is carried on with borrowed capital, the payment of interest to the *rentier*-capitalist will check the progress of economic development. For him the power of private property consists of its ability to extract income without labour and the most important way of so doing is through the charging of interest on loans; a view which led Proudhon to advocate the establishment of an 'exchange bank' which would lead to the abolition of interest and end the exploitative power of property. Of course, Proudhon and Keynes differed sharply, even fundamentally, on many issues, for whereas the former as a representative of petty bourgeois socialism wanted everybody to become a small owner-worker, Keynes stood firmly for the interests of large-scale industrial capital, as witnessed by his stand at the time of the restoration of the Gold Standard in 1925. Like Keynes, however, Proudhon also saw economic instability as associated with the speculative tendencies of financial capital; like Keynes was to at a later date, Proudhon deemed such tendencies to be unnecessary blemishes which could be got rid of by suitable financial reform. (On the relationship of the economics of Keynes and Proudhon, see Dillard 1942.)

In the present century it was Fascism which, while exempting 'productive' (that is, industrial capital) from its attacks, reserved its most vitriolic remarks for the 'parasitic' element within capital, namely banking capital. It should, of course, be stressed that this 'attack' was entirely sham and was for instance dropped immediately the Nazis seized power.

English Economics and the Growth of State Intervention

Keynes undoubtedly occupies centre-stage as the one thinker who attempted to justify the need for state intervention to regulate and try to save twentieth-century capitalism. It is far from being the case however that this century saw the first major intrusion of the state into economic and social matters. Nor was it the case that this intervention flowed from or was initiated by Keynes' theoretical work from the 1930s onwards; it was more the fact that Keynes reflected rather than inspired such a trend. Although Marx sadly never managed to complete his projected work for *Capital* — which was to have included a systematic treatment of the state as the 'epitome of bourgeois society' (I, Preface) — he was by no means oblivious of the crucial, not to say violent, role played by the state in the period of the very emergence of capital as a socio-economic system, the period which he designated as that of 'primitive capital accumulation'. Not least of the state's activities in this turbulent period was to act as an instrument in the violent ruination of petty commodity production, a process written 'in letters of fire and blood', to recall Marx's graphic phrase.

It is however true that when, in the first quarter of the last century, capital eventually took a firm grip on economic relations and the bourgeoisie, after a long and often bitter struggle with the remnants of the feudal aristocracy, finally emerged as undisputed leaders in the development of the productive forces, the state began to interfere less overtly in economic and social matters; this to such an extent that Engels in his celebrated work *The Condition of the Working Class in England* could say: 'Free competition will suffer no limitations, no state supervision; the whole state is but a burden to it. It would reach its highest perfection in a wholly ungoverned anarchic society' (MECW 4: 564).

The fact that capitalism in the nineteenth century felt little or no need for systematic state support was an indication of its strength, a reflection of the undoubtedly true fact that at this stage it was still a progressive social system, which, however acute its contradictions, was still able to develop the productive forces in a manner enabling it to conquer the world in a relatively short space of time. But the point made by Engels must not be exaggerated, or, to be more precise, it must not be misconstrued. He is referring here to a tendency but one which, as in the case of all such tendencies, was never realised, at least to its 'highest perfection', just as the undoubted trend towards monopoly is never realised completely. Even in its classical phase in England, the country where capitalism reached its most intensive development and the one taken by Marx as the 'model' for his theoretical research, the state always retained certain minimal but quite critical functions. These included, amongst others, the provision of an adequate army, police force, civil service, etc. as well as a range of more narrowly economic needs, such as those in the credit sphere where the government acted as guarantor of the banknote issue, as well as itself assuming the role of principal banker.

It is well known that Keynes himself always tried to point up the revolutionary elements in his theoretical work: it was largely of such attempts that the notion of the 'Keynesian revolution' was born. It is understandable that, for pedagogic, expository or whatever purposes, Keynes' leading supporters should also wish to emphasise the gulf separating Keynes' work and its policy implications from that of his predecessors. But Robinson is overstating the case more than a little when she claims,

> For fifty years before 1914 the established economists of the various schools had all been preaching one doctrine, with great self-confidence and pomposity — the doctrine of *laissez-faire*, the beneficial effects of the free play of market forces. In the English-speaking world, in particular, free trade and balanced budgets were all that was required of government policy. Economic equilibrium would always establish itself. The doctrines were still dominant in the 1920s. (Robinson 1972)

Joan Robinson is exaggerating because not only did the nineteenth-century state always undertake certain functions on behalf of capital but there was always present in neoclassical orthodoxy elements of doubt about the beneficence of the results to be obtained from the operation of an unalloyed policy of *laissez-faire*. Exceptions to such a policy were allowed for by otherwise impeccable neoclassical thinkers. As the nineteenth century progressed, capitalist reality revealed in an increasingly sharp form that the approach outlined by Robinson did not correspond to the actual state of affairs. As far as microeconomics was concerned, this was expressed in the palpable fact that free or 'pure' competition, always regarded as a necessary condition for fair imputation, was being steadily eroded by the inexorable growth of monopoly. This was true even in Britain where for a series of historical reasons the 'ideal type' of perfect competition was most nearly met, certainly when compared with the example of Germany where neither perfect competition nor its theoretical expression, neoclassicism, ever established the same degree of pre-eminence as in the case of Britain. Thus although the thesis of a spontaneously equilibrating capitalism on the basis of the free play of supply and demand had taken firm root in orthodox Anglo-Saxon economics, very few economists were unprepared to acknowledge that there were factors at work upsetting such equilibrating tendencies, even though these disturbances were on the whole regarded as an extraneous evil to be exposed and overcome by appropriate action.

In his classic history of economic theory, Joseph Schumpeter — reminding us that Alfred Marshall, although a staunch defender of free trade declared himself opposed to the 'evils of inequality' and favoured a high level of taxation, which was certainly a departure from a pure economic liberalism — sums up the trends at work in economics over the last quarter of the nineteenth century:

> On the whole, the business class still had its way throughout the period, at least up to the beginning of this century, though much more so in the United States than Europe. But its severe confidence in the virtues of *laissez-faire* was gone and its good conscience was going. Hostile forces were growing with which it had to compromise. Still more significant, it grew increasingly willing to compromise and adopt its enemies' views. Economic liberalism thus became riddled with qualifications that sometimes implied surrender of its principles. (Schumpeter 1963: 761)

And what was true of England, the home of economic liberalism, was much more the case in Germany where the majority of economists were subscribers to the doctrine of *Sozialpolitik*. But this trend away from pure *laissez-faire*, towards the advocacy of a greater degree of state intervention did certainly find its reflection in English economics also. Thus at the end of the last century the British economist, Henry Sidgwick, admitting that there was a potential gap between individual and social interests, could declare, in a manner strikingly anticipating the position of Keynes,

> Given the proper circumstances . . . it might be well to allow industry to function without interference. Yet with economic advancement, the propositions of *laissez-faire* would have to be qualified. Numerous exceptions stemmed from the disparities accruing to the individual and those accruing to society. Indeed it could not be demonstrated that the spontaneous efforts of individuals, motivated by self-interest would maximise material welfare. Often a private enterprise occasioned social costs which it shifted to others . . . and frequently increased social costs were exacerbated by such developments as monopoly. (Quoted in Seligman 1963: 446)

Here on Sidgwick's part (similar instances could be cited from Marshall, Pigou and others) was a clear breach of that utilitarianism which, since Bentham onwards, had provided the philosophical basis (such as it was) for conventional economics, with its assertion that there was a complete identity and harmony of interest between the self-seeking individual on the one hand and society on the other. Likewise — although from a different angle — with the Swedish school of political economy for whom perfect competition and the automatic adjustment of markets became in effect legends. The real 'distortions' and 'errors' of the market could be overcome by state action, including action to determine the level of purchasing power. In fact orthodox economics, whatever its theoretical precepts or its underlying philosophical stance might suggest, had never been able entirely to ignore the reality of periodic commodity overproduction which manifested itself even before the first generalised economic crisis — in the case of Britain, in 1825. Even J.-B. Say, for Keynes the doyen of the old discredited classicism, was prepared to allow for the impact of random or subjective factors in bringing about disturbances to an otherwise smoothly operating economic system, such as the defaulting of debtors, the impatience of creditors, or the errors in estimates of the state of the market for goods, etc.

And this same tendency to question the continuing wisdom or relevance of a doctrine which declared state intervention to be in principle a bad thing found its expression in the sphere not merely of economics but also political theory. Thus A.V. Dicey, amongst the leading figures in jurisprudence, writing at the opening of the present century could declare:

> The current of opinion [has] for between thirty and forty years been running with more and more force in the direction of collectivism, with the natural consequence that by 1900 the doctrine of *laissez-faire*, in spite of the large element of truth which it contained, has more or less lost its hold on the English people. (Quoted in McLennan *et al*. 1984: 14)

The point here is that in any economy based on the division of labour and exchange it goes without saying that there must be a market. Amongst the orthodox economists the need for such a market was not, of course, challenged; it turned out however that in practice its nature could vary greatly. In the twentieth century especially the dominant motif of orthodox economics to the effect that there existed a 'fair' distribution of wealth on the basis of a free market came under sustained attack from various quarters, not least from the working class, which from the late 1880s onwards was becoming more extensively organised and was turning increasingly to socialist ideas; orthodoxy was obliged to retreat with its theories of imperfect competition and the 'mixed economy' in which the state was accorded a central role. Keynes' work was an integral part of this accommodation amongst orthodox economics as a whole to the changing reality of capitalist development. The point to be stressed was that it was a reaction to that changing reality and by no means the initiator of such a change, and this must be emphasised in face of the grossly exaggerated role which Keynes assigned to ideas in changing the world.

Did Keynesianism Cause the Post-War Boom?

It goes without saying that Keynesianism has latterly become a dirty word. Not only is the supposed mismanagement of the post-war British economy, about which many now complain, laid at Keynes' door, but he is further held responsible for the ruinous idea of budget deficits which, it is popularly believed, have done much to land us in our current crisis. And, as though this list of charges was not sufficient, Keynes led us not merely to the spurious idea that the economy could be fine tuned but he also opened the door to a baleful state regulation of the economy. These might be considered grave charges; very few of them, if any, can be substantiated. For instance, we have already noted that Keynes explicitly rejected the notion that a series of tiny adjustments in the budgetary aggregates could regulate the economy within any desired limits. The best that might be said here for Keynes' detractors is that certain of his followers may have misinterpreted his work along these lines; this is indeed the complaint of Robinson, Hutchison and others (although Hutchison and Robinson disagree markedly on the nature of these misinterpretations).

But this notwithstanding, two things are beyond dispute. In the first place until the mid-1970s unemployment in the United Kingdom rarely reached 2 per cent, an extremely low figure in the light of William Beveridge's proposal that 3 per cent was a realistic post-war level to be aimed at — a target which Keynes in turn considered improbable of realisation. Second, it was certainly one of the most persistent elements of the conventional wisdom of the 1950s and 1960s that these low unemployment figures and the relative prosperity they entailed were due to the revolution in economic policy for which Keynes had laid the theoretical foundation.

The widely accepted view is that Keynes' long struggle was to convince the strategically placed policy-makers about the wisdom of his proposals together with the theory that underlay them; once this was achieved (after about 1940) the way was clear for a greater degree of state intervention. And, thanks to the final triumph of Keynes' ideas, prosperity after 1945 was maintained, with the implication that it was only from the mid-1970s onwards, when such Keynesian policies were rejected, that the economy plunged into an otherwise avoidable slump. Here clearly the dominance is given to the role of ideas in shaping socio-economic policy. A recent writer has summed up the way in which the issue has usually been regarded:

> our perspective on the 'Keynesian revolution' was delightfully simple; recent economic history tended to be written by economists or historians of economic thought, and both tended to see economic theory as the main force behind economic policy. Economic policy was presented as a clash between entrenched orthodoxy and an intellectually and morally superior force, Keynesianism, which eventually triumphed with the commitment to maintain high stable levels of employment in the 1944 White Paper. (Booth 1983)

Donald Winch would seem to be adopting a similar stance: 'In the light of this experience one might conclude that the Keynesian revolution in

policy has either been supremely successful or that, for other unexplain-
ed reasons, it has proved unnecessary' (Winch 1972: 293)

It is, of course, the case that post-war governments publicly committed themselves to the establishment of a high and stable level of employment. The *White Paper on Employment Policy* (1944) to which Booth refers
was quite explicit on the matter:

> The Government accept as one of their primary aims and respon-
> sibilities the maintenance of a high and stable level of employment
> after the war. . . . Total expenditure on goods and services must be
> prevented from falling to a level where general unemployment appears.

Not only did post-war governments in this and other declarations publicly pledge themselves to a policy of full employment, but they now had
available a state budget which was much larger than before the war. But
these changed circumstances notwithstanding, many writers have cast considerable doubt about whether any government in the post-war period
did in fact ever attempt to regulate the economy according to the conventional Keynesian ideas of budgetary management. [6] Sir Alec Cairncross,
with a minor qualification, appears to support this view:

> The answer is that although Keynesian ideas, by prolonging the post-
> war period of cheap money, undoubtedly contributed to the early
> establishment of full employment, they were rarely put to the test in
> the 1950s and 1960s. Demand was usually tugging at the leash of fiscal
> restraint and the efforts of governments were as concentrated on keep-
> ing inflation in check as in trying to ensure full employment . . .
> throughout the period the central government ran a substantial surplus
> on current account that until 1973 met most of the borrowing re-
> quirements of the nationalised industries. . . . The techniques of de-
> mand management were shot through with Keynesian ideas but demand
> management itself operated on buoyant market forces and even then
> only within narrow limits. (Cairncross, in Floud and McCloskey (eds)
> 1981, vol. 2: 374)

In an earlier and well-known article, R.C.O. Mathews was even more
forthright in repudiating the still widely-held view that it was the operation of Keynesian policies which explain the expansion of capitalism in
the 1950s and 1960s for 'throughout the postwar period the Government,
so far from injecting demand into the system has persistently had a large
current account surplus. . . . Government saving has averaged 3 per cent

of national income' (Mathews 1968).

Mathews proceeds to emphasise the role of private investment as the key to an explanation of the expansion of the economy after 1945: 'the rise of investment must be at the heart of any explanation of the rise in the level of economic activity' (ibid.). But Mathews rejects the idea that it was public investment which was here the key factor (Keynes' 'socialised investment'). On the contrary, he suggests that 'investment in those industries that fall within the public sector now has been a smaller proportion of total investment, than investment in those industries was before the war.' Here Mathews takes a similar position to Cairncross, who also points to the favourable conditions for private investment as constituting a vital factor in the economy of the post-war world. But Cairncross finds little evidence that such investment derived from Keynesian policies of demand management: he stresses the fact that the period after 1945 followed the severest slump in the history of capitalism as well as a war which entailed the widespread physical destruction of capital. Here the situation was quite different from the conditions emerging from the First World War: during that war not only was the destruction of the productive forces, apart from human labour, relatively modest but the war had been preceded by an intensive boom.

Keynesianism and the Inter-War Slump

A persistent complaint from a series of commentators who have considered the current crisis of Keynesianism has proceeded along the following lines: Keynesianism was applied in a post-war world which was quite inappropriate for the sort of economic policy measures which Keynes had advocated. Keynesianism was a policy suitable for conditions of mass unemployment when the running of a budget deficit would have made a considerable contribution to alleviating such a situation. But, it is argued, when it came to fine tuning the economy, along lines proposed by many of Keynes' followers in the post-war years, the matter was of a quite different order, and here Keynesianism proved to be a somewhat blunt and unsuitable instrument.

In the light of this proposition, let us consider the inter-war crisis, especially as it was reflected in the case of British capitalism. To put the issue in the form of a question: Would a Keynesian policy, if attempted, have been successful? Or posing the matter somewhat differently: Was Keynes correct in his oft-repeated contention that the persistence of conditions of slump in the period between the wars in Britain was due to the failure of economic policy? The answer to both these questions must be emphatically in the negative. Given the long-term nature of Britain's industrial malaise in the 1920s — the widely accepted fact that it was a legacy of a past industrial structure and a deeply entrenched relationship with a world economy currently undergoing a major transformation, not least the result of the First World War — it is inconceivable that an organic crisis of the scope and depth which existed throughout the inter-war period could have been even seriously arrested, let alone reversed, by means of either easier monetary conditions or a lower exchange rate (a policy which Keynes, of course, supported). The truth of this proposition is expressed in the fact that when both these conditions were in fact realised after 1931–32 the staple industries (coal, cotton, shipbuilding, etc.) on which the economy as a whole depended for its revival showed little sign of recovery.

Given the evident inadequacy of a purely monetary policy as a means to economic recovery, the only alternative would have been one centred on a considerable increase in government expenditure — the Keynesian solution. Leaving aside the barriers to the implementation of such a policy provided by the conventional wisdom of the time ('sound finance') against which Keynes complained so bitterly and consistently, it is apparent that an increase in government spending of anything remotely approaching the magnitudes needed would in fact have been impossible. It has been calculated (Glynn and Howells 1980) that to restore full employment and generate the near 3 million increase in employment required at the nadir of the Depression would have involved increased government outlays of some £500 million, a figure roughly equivalent to 14 per cent of the 1932 gross domestic product, or nearly half the total public authority spending of that year. It would have implied a rise in spending by the government of some 70 per cent or a reduction in taxation of roughly the same order. 'Even before one asks where the funds to meet the deficit might have come from, the required amount can already be seen to be in the realms of political and economic fantasy' (ibid.).

Not least of the consequences of an attempt to put into action any Keynesian-style policy in the concrete conditions of the early 1930s slump would have been a massive flight of capital from London, the prospect of which haunted the MacDonald government as it agonised over a much smaller budget deficit in the course of 1931. This aside, the financing of a government borrowing requirement on the scale needed could not but have involved a steep rise in interest rates to facilitate a sale of government paper of the proportions required. (Far from suffering euthanasia, the *rentier* would thus have gained greatly from the operation of a

Keynesian-style policy.) Such increased interest rates must have imped-
ed those modest forces towards recovery, not least in the house-building
sector of the economy which has often been pointed to as that area which
derived benefit from the cheap money policy operating after 1932. Further, the effect of a sharp rise in imports which the vast boost in government spending would have entailed must have brought insuperable balance
of payment constraints to the operation of the policy.

Even ignoring these in practice insurmountable problems, it is also
highly dubious whether a generalised reflation of the economy along conventional Keynesian lines could have mopped up the unemployment. As
we have already noted, Keynes himself realised that blanket measures
to reflate the economy were not appropriate as a condition of relative
full employment began to be realised in the run-up to the Second World
War. But the inadequacy of such measures is by no means confined to
conditions where comparatively high levels of employment prevail. This
is so, given the fact that one inherent feature of the capitalist economy,
to which Marxism has traditionally pointed, is its tendency to develop
in an uneven manner, and this is true as much on a national scale as internationally. British capital in the 1920s and 1930s was suffering not merely the effects of a deep cyclical downturn in world economy but as much
from a series of severe structural problems. A deep imbalance in the
economy accumulated from the last quarter of the nineteenth century had
created a situation where the north of the country was suffering acute
depression whilst the south, and especially the London conurbation, was,
by comparison at least, relatively prosperous. Such a chronic imbalance
(one incidentally which persisted throughout the post-war boom and has
now reappeared in acute form) required for its solution not a generalised
boost to demand which a large government deficit would have created
but a fundamental shift in the pattern of investment. An overall consumer-
led fiscal expansion would undoubtedly have resulted in serious
overheating in certain areas of the economy — principally in the south-
east — but could have contributed but marginally to the severely hit regions
in other parts of the country.

Only a highly centralised state-directed economy, along the lines operating in Germany after the victory of Fascism in 1933, and of the sort
advocated in Britain by Mosley and others, could have engineered such
a shift. As the German experience demonstrated, such a system was possible only on the basis of a profound social and political counter-revolution.
And it must also be added that even a Fascist policy could not eliminate
the contradictions of capitalism: it merely raised them to a new pitch
of intensity which amongst other things made world war inevitable.

Keynes and the Break-up of Economic Liberalism

It has been widely noted by historians of economics that several works appeared in the 1930s, each in their own particular way trying to formulate ideas similar in spirit to those of Keynes — a sure manifestation that *The General Theory* marked a definite response to ideas which had already gained a certain resonance amongst economists and politicians in a number of countries. The example of the Swedish school (Myrdal, Ohlin, *et al.*) has often been pointed to in this regard. It was in Sweden that ideas of a broadly Keynesian nature developed in the 1930s; but it is clear that they were not directly inspired by Keynes, for as Myrdal recalls: 'In Sweden, where we grew up in the tradition of Knut Wicksell, Keynes' works were read as interesting and important contributions along the familiar line of thought, but not in any sense as a revolutionary breakthrough' (Myrdal, *Against the Stream: Critical Essays in Economics* (1973), quoted in Garvy 1975). Michal Kalecki, the Polish economist (who, according to Robinson (1962: 93), discovered the General Theory simultaneously with Keynes) is another case of an economist working along the same lines as Keynes, but quite independently of him. Such pervasive theoretical developments, appearing in several countries in the same period, were undoubtedly the reflection of a concrete need: that for a 'new economics' to provide a policy to tackle an apparently intractable world slump. And independently of these theoretical efforts on the part of Keynes, Myrdal, Kalecki and others, such a policy was being groped towards in practice — pragmatically so in the case of the American New Deal. Here again the Keynesian revolution cannot be said to have inspired Roosevelt's programme. As M.S. Eccles, one of Roosevelt's advisers, said of the meetings which hammered out the New Deal:

> With the exception of Ezekiel and Tugwell I doubt whether any of the men in the room had ever heard of John Maynard Keynes, the English economist who has frequently been referred to as the economic philosopher of the New Deal. At least none of them cited his writing to support his own case, and the concepts I formulated, which have been called 'Keynesian' were not abstracted from his books, which I had never read. (Eccles, *Beckoning Frontiers* (1951), Garry (1975).)

Such examples are not only indicative of the world character of the crisis which capitalism faced in the 1930s but provide striking disproof of Keynes' fond belief in the autonomy of ideas as the prime determinant of economic and political programmes. For it must be emphasised that the trend towards Keynesian-type policies was by no means limited to the United States and Britain. We have noted in the case of England that by the close of the nineteenth century dents of a serious nature had already been made in the doctrine of *laissez-faire*, with its prohibition of state interference in economic matters beyond a highly limited sphere (the 'minimum state'). It was however in Nazi Germany after 1933 and before *The General Theory* appeared that a Keynesian-style policy involving a considerable state (military) spending programme was put into operation. [7] Because of its delayed economic and social development and its therefore equally tardy entry into the world capitalist market, economic liberalism never exercised the influence in Germany that it did in Britain. The German historical school, for instance, always assigned to the state a central role in securing a future for German capital against its internal and external enemies alike. Hence its repudiation of the doctrine of free trade and its advocacy of tariffs as a necessary instrument in the protection of a still-infant and relatively weak German industry. In this respect it is interesting to remember that Keynes moved sharply towards support for protectionist measures in the 1930s, although he lacked the conviction to advocate outright autarchy, as did the more extreme proponents of protectionism. But the direction of his thought is unmistakable. As Keynes himself records, he was brought up to respect free trade 'not only as an economic doctrine which a rational and instructed person could not doubt but almost as a part of the moral law' (JMK CW 21: 236). But by the 1930s he was able to say, 'I sympathise with those who would minimise, rather than maximise, economic entanglement between nations' (ibid.). This point is even more sharply put elsewhere:

> I am not persuaded that the economic advantages of the international division of labour to-day are at all comparable with what they were. . . . Over an increasingly wide range of industrial, and perhaps of agricultural products also, I become doubtful whether the economic cost of national self-sufficiency is great enough to outweigh the other advantages of gradually bringing the producer and consumer within the ambit of the same national, economic and financial organisation. Experience accumulates to prove that most modern mass-production processes can be performed in most countries and climates with almost equal efficiency (ibid.).

In the view expressed here Keynes was merely reflecting a deep crisis engulfing bourgeois thought. In the nineteenth century, economics had taught that the greatest factor in the production of wealth was the international division of labour; by the 1930s it had discovered that this self-same world division of labour was one of the most potent sources of economic breakdown and crisis. Similarly with the rejection of the Gold Standard which took place in the same decade. In the nineteenth century, gold, as a universal measure of value, became the foundation of all the major monetary systems and as such was supported by all the leading figures in the school of liberal economics. Keynes' well-known denunciation of it as a 'barbarous relic' was again part of a universal trend towards the attempt at 'national' monetary systems, the analogue of the increasingly strident demands for protectionism.

Keynesianism formed one of the main ideological components of post-1945 social democracy, particularly in Britain. But there is nothing intrinsic to Keynesianism that links it of necessity to a reformist–liberal trend, such as social democracy. This, it should be stressed, does not concern Keynes' own explicit politics which, in so far as he identified himself with the 'educated bourgeoisie', were of a generally liberal character. We are dealing rather with the implications (the 'logic' so to speak) of Keynes' economic thought and its relationship to the organic requirements of modern capitalism. In the light of what has been noted above both about Keynes' attitude to previously hallowed ideas such as free trade and the Gold Standard, as well as the rejection of these doctrines in Germany, it is noteworthy that amongst those who advocated Keynesian-type policies in the 1920s, before they were given a degree of respectability by the publication of *The General Theory*, was Sir Oswald Mosley. In a chequered political career, Mosley was, amongst other things, a junior minister in the 1929 MacDonald government and later leader of the British Fascist movement. Mosley's plan to deal with the mounting unemployment crisis, presented to the MacDonald government in 1930, was based on a combination of Keynesian-style state spending programmes and protectionist measures to shelter British capitalism from the gale of world competition. (Mosley saw in the empire a potential trading bloc to which British exports would have privileged access.) Robert Skidelsky, biographer of both Keynes and Mosley, puts the relationship between their thinking as follows:

> Mosley was a disciple of Keynes in the 1920s and in one important respect . . . Mosley's Fascism was distinctively English. It is a paradox, but not perhaps a surprising one, that out of the heart of economic liberalism should have come its most sustained and brilliant critic: that body of economic doctrine associated with the name of Keynes. Mosley was a disciple of Keynes in the 1920s; and

Keynesianism was his great contribution to Fascism. It was Keynesianism which in the last resort made Mosley's Fascism distinctively English, though it was not an Englishness which most English pundits were then prepared to recognise, being as remote from the Keynesian thinking as they were from the problems which gave birth to it. (Skidelsky 1975: 302)

Like Keynes, Mosley also argued that production was suffering at the hands of the financiers and bankers, a view which in the case of the Fascist Mosley had the effect of putting industrial capital and the working class on the same side against the 'parasitic' financiers. And, as Skidelsky points out, this same idea is present in Keynes:

> . . . curiously enough Keynes did not include the class struggle [between capitalists and workers] in his account of interest conflicts. He tended to assume an identity of interest between workers and manufacturers against their common enemy — the *rentier* and banker. This notion of the conflict of interest within the capitalist community and the identity of interest between the workers and one section of that community — the manufacturers — was to have a profound influence on Mosley's thought. It was to give him both a strategy and a philosophy quite different from the standard socialist conception of a struggle in which the workers were all on one side, and the wicked capitalists all on the other. Henceforth the producers' state would be the goal; and finance the enemy. (ibid.: 141)

Keynes made the point that under conditions of free trade and capital movements the desired fall in interest rates would be impossible to achieve. Indeed, according to Keynes himself, the economic policies implicit in *The General Theory*, far from being inimical to the needs of a Fascist economy were, if anything, easier to operate than in a regime based on parliamentary democracy of the sort Keynes assumed in existence while the book had been prepared. In the preface to the German edition of *The General Theory* we find Keynes making the following observation:

> I confess that much of the following book is illustrated and expounded mainly with reference to the conditions existing in the Anglo-Saxon countries. Nevertheless the theory of output as a whole, which is what the following book purports to provide, is much more easily adapted to the conditions of a totalitarian state [*totaler staat*, Keynes' euphemism for the Fascism which had then installed itself in Germany] than is the production and distribution of a given output produced under

conditions of perfect competition and a large measure of *laissez-faire*. This is one of the reasons that justifies my calling my theory a general theory. Since it is based on less narrow asumptions than the orthodox theory, it is also more easily adapted to a large order of different circumstances. Although I have thus worked it out having the conditions in the Anglo-Saxon countries in view — where a great deal of *laissez-faire* still prevails — it yet remains applicable in situations where national leadership is more pronounced. (see Schefold 1980)

This chapter has been concerned with certain aspects of the Keynesian revolution. We have tried to place this revolution in its historical and social context, to see it as a reflection of the development of the economy itself in a period when capitalism had long since ceased to be a progressive force, and as such could no longer rely upon its inherent strength but had increasingly to depend upon the bourgeois state as it grappled with a series of economic, political and social crises on a national and international level. From this viewpoint there was nothing 'progressive' about Keynes' ideas, despite the efforts of his more radical followers in the post-war years to present them as such. In the field of economic theory Keynes, by explicit choice, was a follower of the principal initiator of the school of vulgar political economy, the reactionary Malthus, as against Ricardo, whose work constitutes one of the enduring achievements of early nineteenth-century bourgeois thought and in the case of economics its single most enduring achievement. As far as economic policy goes, Keynes came to base himself on a narrow and reactionary economic nationalism which repudiated the greatest single achievement of capitalism: the establishment of a world market and an international division of labour.

That the state must be responsible for 'planning' the economy; that is must assure an abundance of 'cheap money' (low interest rates); that free trade is a prejudice which if necessary must be abandoned — all these ideas contain more than an echo of mercantilist doctrines. That Keynes, widely regarded by friend and foe alike as the outstanding economist of the century, was not only unable to make a single advance over the work of the great classical economists (Smith and Ricardo) but was driven to revert to several of the key ideas of an economic theory, mercantilism, which appeared finally to have faded out by the end of the eighteenth century, is but an expression of the historical character of the crisis gripping economics as a whole in the present century. As to Keynes' not immodest claim that he had effected a revolution in economic theory which in particular would destroy 'the Ricardian foundations of Marxism', this will be the subject of the next chapter.

Notes

1. One cannot, therefore, accept Joan Robinson's confident assertion (1962: 74) about Keynes: 'First of all, Keynes brought back something of the hard-headedness of the Classics. He saw the capitalist system as a system, a going concern, a phase in historical development.' It was precisely a view of capitalism as a definite mode of production, arising under definite historical conditions, which was missing in Keynes.

2. This does not mean that the polemic between the advocates of monetary and fiscal policy is entirely devoid of importance. In practice, fiscal policy is concerned with the redistribution of the national income, the forcible taking by the state of part of the social value from its original owners and its use for ends which the government itself decides upon. As against this, monetary policy is essentially state credit policy. On the theoretical level, in relation to their theory of money, the Keynesians and the monetarists have much in common. Both start from the point of view of the individual as the basic unit of the economy: when such individuals are aggregated we arrive at the demand for money. Amongst other things this involves a central confusion between money acting as a means of exchange and money functioning as capital (money capital). We shall return to this point in the next chapter.

3. In reviewing *The General Theory*, Roll made the following point: 'it is significant that many of the advances in the theory of imperfect competition are due to Italian and German economists who uphold the doctrines of Fascism. The examination of limited competition made by one of these leads its author to the conclusion that the achievement of equilibrium in the increasingly unstable conditions of to-day is the function of the state. Like the Italian economist Amoroso, he regards the corporative state as the ideal machinery for this purpose. Mr Keynes' doctrine on money, interest and government control of investment also have their counterparts, if not in Fascist theory, at any rate in Fascist practice. However much the economic policy of Germany and Italy may vary from the detailed form in which Mr Keynes would like the policy to be cast, a good case can be made out for saying that Fascist policy is based on some of his principles' (Roll 1938). Keynes' ideas were certainly well received in Nazi economic journals such as *Der deutsche Volkswirt* and *Die deutsche Volkwirtschaft*.

4. Underconsumptionists, such as Hobson, saw the remedy to slump as lying in savings which would transfer income from accumulation (the capitalists) to the consumers (the workers). Keynes took the problem facing capitalism to be a lack of credit which was itself the result of a restrictive financial policy. In times of slump this created a deficiency of investment: the remedy was to raise the level of investment by means of a 'cheap money' policy and, should this prove inadequate, by means of state enterprise.

5. 'Malthus is interested not in concealing the contradictions of bourgeois production, but on the contrary, in emphasising them, on the one hand in order to prove that the poverty of the working classes is necessary (as it is, indeed, for this mode of production) and, on the other hand, to demonstrate to the capitalists the necessity for a well-fed Church and State hierarchy in order to create an adequate demand for the commodities they produce' (Th III: 57). But while Malthus drew attention to certain of capitalism's contradictions he shied away from probing to their essence in the conflict of labour and capital.

6. Joan Robinson says somewhat casually of post-war Keynesian policy: 'As we know, for twenty-five years serious recessions were avoided by following this policy' (Robinson 1972). Such a simple judgement would now fail to find anything near unanimous support.

7. In an interesting article, George Garvy (1975) draws attention to the abortive efforts of prominent figures in pre-Hitler Germany, including W.S. Woytinsky, statistician for the German Trade Union Federation, to enlist Keynes' support for a reflationary policy which they hoped would stave off Fascist dictatorship. But as Robinson (1973) plaintively remarks, 'Hitler had already found out how to cure unemployment before Keynes had finished explaining why it occurred.' As Garvy notes, 'No more than Roosevelt did Hitler have to await the publication of *The General Theory* to embark on expansionary policies,

even though the German edition followed the original by only a few months. G. Strasser [leader of the so-called 'left-wing' of the Nazi Party who had urged the policy of credit-creation for 'productive' purposes in the period prior to 1933], G. Feder and others in Hitler's party had already offered the prescriptions.' And he adds, 'It was [Hitler] who put into effect, by means of a massive rearmament programme, the basic ideas of those of his opponents who saw in an active job-creating counter-cyclical policy the only way for preserving German democracy.'

3 THE FOUNDATION OF KEYNES' ECONOMICS

To historians of economic theory the triumph of the neoclassical synthesis should appear as most inappropriate, for the basis of Keynes's formal training in the economics of Ricardo and Marshall left a strong imprint on his own contributions to economic theory. It would seem more appropriate to link Keynes's own theory with the long-period theory of the classical political economists. The possibility of such a relation has become obvious with the post-Keynesian contribution of a long-period theory based on Keynes's short-period theory which closely resembled, in both content and concern, the classical theory of Ricardo and Marx. (Kregel 1975: xv)[1]

This chapter explores certain aspects of the relationship between the economic theories of Karl Marx and J.M. Keynes from one particular angle, that of the underlying methodologies and general conceptions of these two economic theorists. And because of its importance in current analyses of the Keynesian crisis, we intend to explore these matters from one specific angle: from the standpoint of those who wish to create a new political economy on the basis of a fusion of certain strands within Keynesian economics on the one hand, and some elements from the Marxist–classical tradition on the other. Such efforts involve two distinct, although related questions:
1. That concerning the relationship of the political economy of the classical school to that of Marx. Keynes himself certainly believed that his new economics would undermine what he called the Ricardian foundations of Marxism. In other words, he identified the classical political economy of Ricardo with Marx's critique of it. We have already commented on this issue and can therefore be brief. Marx's work involved a critique of political economy, one which understood that there were a series of flaws, fatal in the final analysis, associated with the work of even the best representatives of the school; it was these flaws which made it vulnerable to the attacks of the vulgar, commonplace writers who emerged in the period following Ricardo's death. (The best treatment of the transition from classical to vulgar economics is provided by Rubin (1979).) The collapse of Ricardian economics was not an event explicable in ideological terms only. That is to say, while Ricardo's doctrines were certainly attacked because of the subversive uses to which they were being

put, not least by the various radical writers in the 1820s and 1830s, the fact remains that the opponents of the classical school did have definite weaknesses in Ricardo's economics at which to aim their fire and no amount of formal rearranging of the categories of that economics could protect it from its vulgar detractors. Only a fundamental reworking of classical economics which truly transcended it (that is, preserved its positive features while disposing of its negative aspects) could produce a real development of this tradition. It fell to Marx's lot to make precisely this advance. It is from this standpoint that those attempts made by certain post-Keynesians, as well as by several Marxists, to conflate the work of classical economists and that of Marx are at base erroneous and must be rejected.

2. The second issue implicit in the efforts to reconstitute political economy along lines proposed by Kregel and others involves a certain view of the relationship of Keynes' work to the classical tradition. In exploring the foundations of Keynes' economics we shall be concerned with this latter question. Briefly, to anticipate the line of argument, we shall suggest that at a fundamental level these two traditions have little in common and that Keynesian economics is, in the last resort, a continuation, under twentieth-century conditions to be sure, of the vulgar tradition in political economy. We intend to defend this proposition by means of an examination of the categories of *The General Theory*, suggesting that their subjective and psychological character expresses clearly that they do indeed derive from the vulgar school and not from that represented by Petty, Smith, Ricardo and others.

As we have already seen, the whole of the post-war period has witnessed something of a struggle for the soul of Keynes. On the one hand, in the case of the 'neoclassical synthesis', efforts were made to incorporate the teachings of Keynes into the body of neoclassical orthodoxy, producing what Robinson variously castigated as a 'bastard' or 'bowdlerised' Keynesianism. From a quite different standpoint, equally persistent attempts have been made to bring together certain elements from Keynes' work with aspects of the classical–Marxian tradition. We shall be concerned not with those who sought to marry the work of Keynes to the prevailing neoclassical orthodoxy but with these latter efforts in order to examine whether, in principle, they are soundly based.

There is no doubt that the emergence of Keynesianism in the 1930s and its later rise to a position of almost unchallenged dominance in the post-war period exercised a decisive influence upon many Marxists operating within the field of economics. Because this is not our prime concern, the historical references will not be explored; but in brief the

following can be asserted: under the impact of prevailing Keynesian orthodoxy many Marxists were inclined to read *Capital* and other of Marx's
economic works from the standpoint of some version or other of an underconsumptionist theory of capitalist breakdown. That is to say they were
inclined, as were certain of Keynes' followers, to see the principal problem for capitalism as lying in a tendency for consumption to fall below
the level of that required to sustain investment and full employment, particularly the full employment of labour. The corollary of this position
was that appropriate state action, particularly action associated with the
state budget, could, by raising the level of consumption, overcome this
deficiency.

A book such as Baran and Sweezy's *Monopoly Capital* (1966) is a
striking case in point. In its overall approach this work is Keynesian,
concentrating as it does on what the authors take to be the critical problem for capitalism in the post-war period: the disposal of a rising economic
surplus. According to Baran and Sweezy, the big monopoly and near-
monopoly concerns are able to fix the prices of their output in such a
way as to ensure for themselves ever greater surpluses. This being so,
the problem for capitalism boils down to finding ways to absorb this
surplus. They see such things as increased advertising expenditures, the
economic activities of the state and growing expenditure on arms as the
principal means whereby capitalism disposes of its economic surpluses.
For them the contradictions of capitalism, especially that between the
capitalist class and the working class, no longer exist as they did in Marx's
time. Capitalism is condemned not as an historically limited and inherently
contradictory system but as one subjected to increasing irrationality. In
this way Baran and Sweezy find redundant the basic categories of Marx's
political economy. Thus of the tendency for capitalism to generate a rising economic surplus they say:

> This law immediately invites comparison, as it should, with the
> classical–Marxian law of the falling tendency of the rate of profit.
> Without entering into an analysis of the different versions of the latter,
> we can say that all presuppose a competitive system. By substituting
> the law of rising surplus for the law of falling profit we are therefore
> not rejecting or revising a time-honoured theorem of political economy:
> we are simply taking account of the undoubted fact that the structure
> of the capitalist economy has undergone a fundamental change since
> that theorem was formulated. What is most essential about the change
> from competitive to monopoly capitalism finds its theoretical expres-
> sion in this substitution. [2]

Their book, published in the middle of the inflationary boom, was an indication of the impact which the prevailing Keynesian orthodoxy had on Marxism.

But the seeds of this move towards Keynesianism had been laid long before — in fact in the 1930s, the decade when Keynes' major work first appeared. It is noteworthy that Maurice Dobb, for long undoubtedly the leading commentator on Marxist political economy in England, in introducing Sweezy's earlier and influential exposition of the principles of Marxian economics, *The Theory of Capitalist Development*, to English readers admits that he had himself moved closer to Sweezy's heavy emphasis on underconsumptionism as the major factor explaining capitalist crisis, a move which is reflected in much of Dobb's later writing.

In what is probably still the most satisfactory popular treatment of Marxist political economy, Sweezy had, in this earlier work, when speaking of Keynes as the leading representative of those arguing for liberal capitalist reform, proposed that the critique of such ideas should start 'not from their economic logic but rather from their faulty (usually implicit) assumptions about the relationship, or perhaps one should say lack of relationship, between economics and political action' (Sweezy 1946: 346). Sweezy is making an important point here, namely, that the question at issue is not so much the economic theory of Keynes but rather the false conception which, as a liberal, he held about the relationship of the economic to the political sphere within the capitalist system. The implication is that Keynesian-type economics was sound in the abstract: the problem arose when one attempted to implement such economics in the 'real world', in the face of a state which was not impartial as between social forces and therefore not neutral about policy prescriptions. Keynes is to be rejected not on theoretical grounds, but from the point of view of pragmatism, namely that his 'solutions' to the ills of capitalism do not in fact work in practice. [3]

It should be noted in passing that this attitude of Sweezy towards Keynes is remarkably similar to that which Keynes himself took to the work of his predecessors: that it was the faulty assumptions rather than the internal logic of the Manchester School which fatally vitiated its work. Thus, 'Our criticism of the accepted theory of economics has consisted not so much in finding logical flaws in its analysis as in pointing out that its tacit assumptions are seldom or never satisfied, with the result that it cannot solve the economic problems of the actual world' (GT: 378).

In our opinion, the position adopted by Sweezy marks a fundamental and wholly unwarranted concession to Keynes. In this chapter we shall suggest that, contrary to Sweezy's view, the 'economic logic' of Keynes was indeed faulty and fatally so; consequently a consideration of this 'economic logic' must form the starting point of any sustained Marxist critique of Keynesianism. And this in turn implies that those efforts on the part of 'left Keynesians' such as Joan Robinson, to effect some theoretical reconciliation between Marx and Keynes are at base misconceived. The critical distinction drawn by Marx between the classical and the vulgar schools in economics provides a decisive conceptual prism through which to examine certain aspects of Keynes' economics. For Marx (I, 81) what he dubbed the vulgar school was concerned only with the most superficial aspects of capitalist economy; at a certain point it was a school which degenerated into apologetics, attempting as it did to rationalise away the contradictions of the capitalist system. [4] In particular, Marx castigated the fetishism inherent in vulgar political economy: the tendency to ascribe social powers and functions to things: for instance to attribute the entrepreneur's ability to make a profit to the natural objects which make up the means of production. [5] We therefore propose to review the main aspects of Keynes' theoretical system from the point of view of Marx's distinction between classical and vulgar political economy.

We can start by pointing to certain key features of Keynes' work which have a direct bearing upon the philosophical and methodological bases of that work. From where, in general, does Keynes begin his analysis? He accepted the fact that capitalism in no way automatically guarantees full employment; there is no self-adjusting mechanism which generates a level of effective demand sufficient to ensure the full utilisation of resources. Keynes' argument runs along the following well-known lines. In the short run — for him the period of greatest concern, although not necessarily so for many of his post-war followers — the level of employment is a function of the level of output which is in turn a function of the level of effective demand. It is this concept, that of effective demand, which is in reality Keynes' key idea, a point widely accepted, certainly amongst his orthodox followers (e.g. Patinkin *et al.*). Effective demand is that demand backed by expenditure. Total expenditure and total sales (assuming no stocks) are the same thing as output. So output is determined by effective demand. Keynes proceeded to break down effective demand into two components — consumption and investment — and analysed each in turn. The basis of the distinction is that money spent on goods and services by individuals to satisfy their own wants is consumption; money spent by enterprises on buildings and machinery in order to produce goods and services in the future is investment. Or, regarding the matter from the standpoint of output, the division is one between investment goods (buildings, machinery, etc.) and consumer goods. To know what determines the level of output — and hence the level of employment — one needs to know what determines the level of consumption and the level of investment. In order to analyse fluctuations in the level of effective demand, Keynes makes use of his three fundamental operational categories — the propensity to consume, the marginal efficiency of capital, and the rate of interest. In combination, these three factors set the limits within which the capitalist economy oscillates, and we shall say more of them presently.

No attempt is made in what follows to provide a full and systematic critique of Keynes' work. Only a few aspects will be touched upon. It is intended to look briefly at certain of Keynes' key concepts, to explore their underlying assumptions, concentrating particularly on Keynes' notion of capital and its 'productivity'. In view of her central role in the interpretation of both Marx and Keynes, brief comment is made towards the end of the chapter about the work of Joan Robinson. But first the overall approach of Marx to the analysis of capitalism can be sketched out in order to highlight the quite different methodological premises from which his work commences.

For Marx the dynamics of capitalism, the search for the 'law of motion of modern society' ('The ultimate aim of this work is to lay bare the law of motion of modern society' — Preface: I) involves as one of its central tasks the investigation of the concept of capital. Despite the claims of empiricism to the contrary, every science has its own hierarchy of concepts; empirical research and individual theories always rest on certain fundamental ideas, forming the cornerstone of the particular department of knowledge concerned. This empiricism denies: it claims to commence from 'the facts', unmediated by any preconceptions. This is however pure illusion: all thought begins from definite concepts as to the nature of its object; in this case the capitalist economy. But whether this starting point is a conscious one or not is a matter not without its importance. For those who start with unconscious theoretical categories — that is, from categories which have not been arrived at on the basis of a real critical assimilation of all the past developments in the science concerned — inevitably start their operations from the most vulgar, commonplace definitions. Keynes was here no exception to this law of thought. As we shall see, he did in fact employ an implicit definition of capital and of capitalism, namely as a system of production which was aimed at the satisfaction of human needs. His objection to this system lay in the fact that in its twentieth-century form (where monopoly dominated) it was not doing this as effectively as it could.

There is no doubt that in the case of economic theory the most basic concept with which it deals is that of capital. One of Marx's most persistent criticisms of the classical school was that it had no real, worked-out, truly consistent concept of capital. Even for Ricardo, the best of the classical economists, capital was merely 'stored up labour', a notion which had the effect of making capital coeval with human existence in the sense that even the most primitive tool of the savage represents 'stored up labour', the result of past effort on his part, and therefore for Ricardo capital. The seeming universality and general applicability of such an idea was gained, Marx held, at the expense of any real concrete historical content. This is made clear in Marx's comments on the economists' conception of capital:

> Capital consists of raw materials, instruments of labour and means of subsistence of all kinds, which are utilised in order to produce new raw materials, instruments of labour and new means of subsistence. All these are component parts, are creations of labour, products of labour, accumulated labour. Accumulated labour which serves as a new means of production is capital.
>
> So say the economists.
>
> What is a Negro slave? A man of the black race. The one explanation is as good as the other.
>
> A Negro is a Negro. He only becomes a slave under certain relationships. A cotton spinning machine is a machine for spinning cotton. Only in certain relationships does it become capital. Torn from these relationships it is no more capital than gold is itself money or sugar the price of sugar. (*Wage Labour and Capital*)

According to Marx, the vulgar economists had an even shallower and fetishistic view of capital. Now the connection between capital and labour in the economics which emerged following the disintegration of the Ricardian school (*c.* 1830) was entirely lost sight of: the reward to the holders of capital was hereafter held to be a reward for their abstinence or waiting. The unwritten assumption in this view was that capitalism was a system designed to produce wealth for consumption and that those who delayed such consumption had to be appropriately rewarded. Any historical analysis of capital, any inkling that it might express economic relations specific to certain periods and conditions only, fell quite outside the theoretical vision of neoclassical economics.

The Commonplace View of Capital

The outcome of this trend can be seen when we look at the contemporary idea of capital present in orthodox economics. As an example we take the definition of capital offered by the 1984 edition of the *Penguin Dictionary of Economics*, a summary of similar notions to be found in a hundred textbooks:

> The stock of goods which are used in production and which have themselves been produced. . . . The word capital in economics generally means real capital — that is physical goods. . . . Two important features of capital are (a) that its creation involves a sacrifice, since resources are devoted to making non-consumable capital goods instead of goods for immediate consumption, and (b) that it enhances the PRODUCTIVITY of the FACTORS OF PRODUCTION, LAND AND LABOUR; it is the enhanced productivity which represents a reward for the sacrifice involved in creating capital. (Bannock *et al.* 1984: 61)

Two points arise from this definition. (a) Capital is a 'thing' merely and not a social relation of production. As such it is presumably coeval with man, indeed perhaps even with the animal kingdom. This was a view which led to a series of strange conclusions and ones which gave Marx much pleasure; [6] (b) despite its seeming lack of social content, this definition does in point of fact carry a very specific conception of the capitalist mode of production. For the reward to capital, the sacrifice of owning it, arises from the fact that immediate consumption must be postponed. Here, implicitly, is the notion that capitalism is a system founded on the satisfaction of human requirements, a system dedicated to providing for the needs of 'the consumer'. Marx rejected such a petty bourgeois notion because it obscured the fact that under capitalism the aim of production is, and can only be, the self-expansion of capital, that is, its continual accumulation.

Now it is, of course, a truism to say that Keynes criticised certain aspects of the work of the neoclassical school of his day, just as others had done prior to him. But it is equally the case that such criticisms never achieved the rank of anything fundamental, never probed to the epistemological foundations of this school, never inquired into the historical and social conceptions which underlay it. On the contrary, it is apparent that Keynes' work was itself imbued with precisely the same anti-historical conceptions which predominated in neoclassical economics.

For as is well known, Keynes deliberately abstracts himself from any critical analysis of the social structure of society and its laws of development. In other words, he takes the capitalist system for granted, accepts its appearances as constituting its essence. His concern is exclusively with the functioning rather than the dynamics of capitalism. In his theoretical system he takes both the productive forces and the relations of production to be immutable elements, given once and for all: 'We take as given the existing skill and quantity of available labour, the existing quantity and quality of equipment, the existing technique, the degree of competition . . . as well as the social structure including the forces, other than our variables . . . which determine the distribution of the national income' (GT: 245). Elsewhere Keynes writes that he takes as given (that is, as fixed) the entire 'economic framework' of capitalism (GT: 246).

Now, of course, the fact that Keynes took these factors as 'given' does not mean that he was innocent of the fact that, in the empirical sense, this was not the case. A far more serious issue is involved here. It reveals the fact that Keynes' work involved the conventional and essentially positivist process of model-building whereby, on the basis of a series of arbitrary assumptions, a model of the economy is constructed. That is, Keynes makes a series of assumptions in order to simplify the analysis of the economy — such that there is no technical change taking place, that the 'economic framework' of capitalism is fixed — and on the basis of these abstractions a coherent picture of the world is derived. But, as in the case of the traditional assumption of perfect competition, such abstractions are purely mental devices having no basis in the reality of the phenomena being investigated. And precisely because of this they must be arbitrary and subjective. Marx's analysis is of course based on abstractions ('In the analysis of economic forms, moreover, neither microscopes nor chemical reagents are of use. The force of abstraction must replace both.' Preface: I) but his are abstractions of a quite different order, reflecting as they do the real movement of capital. (For an excellent exposition of Marx's method of abstraction in *Capital* and the difference between his procedure and that employed by positivism, see Ilyenkov (1979).)

For Marx all real economic categories — capital, value, rent, interest, profit, etc. — reflect not a series of arbitrary mental assumptions but definite social relations of production. Consequently, they are not categories valid for all epochs and all societies. Let us take the example of capital. According to Marx, capital is no mere thing — raw materials, buildings, factories, etc. — but a social relation which finds expression in or attaches itself to many different things such as money or commodities. The central feature of capitalism, its *specifica differentia*, the quality which marks it off from past economic systems, is that the means of production are monopolised by a class and face another class, the working class, which is obliged out of necessity to sell its ability to work (in Marx's terminology, its labour power) to one or other owner of capital. This is why for Marx the essence of capital lies in the fact that it is a social relation and not merely a material thing. Just as the examination of a sack of wheat cannot disclose the social relations under which it was produced (in a feudal demesne, by slave labour, on a collective farm, etc.) so the natural properties of the means of production can never tell us whether they function as capital. A certain class of people may own things such as factories, financial assets and so on but only a definite social process transforms these things into instruments of exploitation, converts them into bearers of that social relationship which Marx designates by the term 'capital'. Capital is a specific, historically defined, social relation of production. By a fetishistic notion of capital Marx meant precisely that view which tended to ascribe to objects qualities which it was imagined flowed from the material properties of such objects but which in point of fact arose entirely and exclusively from the social role occupied by these things in the process of material production. The notion that things are productive by their nature rather than by virtue of the specific place they occupy in a definite network of social relations was precisely the fetishistic view of capital to which Marx objected.

In its most general form (leaving aside its various types) capital is depicted by Marx in the schema $M-C-C'-M'$ (M representing the initial sum of money owned by the capitalist). Ignoring here its actual origin, this sum of money is thrown into production, being used initially to purchase commodities, C, including the commodity labour power. In the process of production these commodities are in turn transformed into ones involving a greater amount of (potential) value, C', which are then sold for an equivalent sum of money, M'. It is from this latter sum of money, M', that the capitalist meets his individual consumption needs but much more crucially it provides the means for the further accumulation of capital — the reconversion of the surplus value embodied in M' back into capital.

This schema, $M-C-C'-M'$, represents in conceptual form the only axis on which production within capitalism takes place. For Marx, capitalism can never be understood if it is seen merely as the production of things satisfying human needs. Were this the case, the limits to production would be purely technical, concerned with the best, most rational, most 'economic' allocation of certain material means to the satisfaction of a number of needs. But to envisage the process of production in this way is to ignore the crucial question of the social framework within which production takes place. For capital, its most vital need is to expand M into M'. As Marx says, this is like the law of Moses; should human needs be met in the process of the self-expansion of capital (as of course within limits they are) this is an incidental matter.

This sketch of Marx's concept of capital reveals, I believe, that he and Keynes approach the analysis of capitalism from quite distinct angles and with fundamentally opposed logics. For although Keynes and Marx both deal in aggregates (in this respect both stand opposed to the old neoclassical approach with its prime focus of interest being the individual), the nature of these aggregates is of a different order. Marx's principal concern is the total social capital (M–C–M') and its subdivisions; Keynes' prime interest lies with effective demand and its chief components, investment and consumption.

If the examination of the capitalist process of production proceeds from the standpoint of Marx, it will be immediately evident that the size of the various revenues which in sum constitute the national income depends essentially upon the size of the total social capital and its rate of turnover in the production process. If, for instance, more capital is employed, if more money is transformed from money into commodities needed for production, more will, other things remaining equal, be advanced as variable capital; that is, as wages. In other words, it is the expansion of capital which increases the mass of labour power employed. The empiricist, because he merely records the 'facts' has no way of comprehending this process theoretically. The reverse of the real relationship could seem to hold: it could just as well be that if more money is spent on variable capital (wages) more capital will result. Indeed this is exactly how the matter does at first sight appear. 'It is the absolute movements of the accumulation of capital which are reflected as relative movements of the mass of exploitable labour power, and therefore seem produced by the latter's own independent movement' (I: 620). And what is true of wages is true equally of all forms of income — profits, rent, interest, etc. The size of these revenues is limited (determined) by the accumulation of capital, and not the other way round. It is not the size of revenues that fixes the size of the total social capital but the latter which determines the former. To begin one's analysis with the conditions which determine the turnover of capital is to start from the inner determining source of the movement of the entire capitalist economy. This movement of social capital does of course reveal itself in the size and movement of the various forms of revenue. But to start with these revenues is to commence from a series of immediate, everyday phenomena as they present themselves on the surface of society. And this was just the central point of Marx's strictures against the school of vulgar economy, namely that it did start uncritically from the immediate economic relations as they appeared on the surface of society. There was no scrutiny of these phenomena to establish their origin, to demonstrate that their roots lay in the specific social relations of a definite economic system, capitalism. The procedure of the vulgar economist did, however, from the point of ideology, carry one advantage: it allowed all the revenues (wages, profits, interest) to be considered of the same status, as 'factor incomes' as they say.

To turn specifically to the case of Keynes: a fall in national income will, in the normal run of things, produce a drop in the level of employment; but this merely raises a deeper, more fundamental question: What brings about the initial fall in income? What is the inner (relatively hidden) source of this outer movement? It is this question which, says Marx, any serious analysis of capitalism and its crises must seek to answer. But it is a question which empiricism says does not admit of an answer — a search for the inner causes of phenomena is in the last resort deemed futile. According to Marx, the essence of capitalist crises, despite the many differing forms which such crises necessarily take, consists of a break in the conditions of capital turnover, a break in the circuit M–C–C'–M'. The movement of capital is the crucial thing from which all else derives and the laws governing the movement of the aggregate capital are the fundamental laws of economics. That is why Marx held that confusion about the nature of capital must lead to confusion about all the other categories of the economy.

Revenue and Capital

The point raised here, the angle from which an analysis of the capitalist economy should begin, is a matter which has continually concerned economics in the past. Let us take the case of Adam Smith. As is widely perceived, Smith held two contradictory theories of value. In places Smith holds to the idea that the value of a commodity is determined by one thing and one thing alone: the quantity of labour embodied in such a commodity. On many occasions, however, he proposed what Dobb and others have appropriately characterised as an adding-up theory of value in which the various forms of revenue (wages, profits, rent) were held, in their summation, to determine the value of the commodity. The conclusion of this latter conception of value is, as Marx puts it, 'that commodity value is composed of various kinds of revenue, or alternatively "resolved into" these revenues, so that it is not the revenues that consist of commodity value but rather the commodity value that consists of revenues' (II: 465). Here Marx is raising precisely the same fundamental question as that involved in a critique of Keynes: In the analysis of capitalism, does one begin from value and capital or from price and income (revenue)?

This duality in Smith constituted an unresolved contradiction in his theoretical work: on one hand the effort to discover the inner workings of the economy (here lay the truly classical element in his work), and on the other a mere registering or cataloguing of economic phenomena (here according to Marx are to be found the seeds of the vulgar strand in Smith). Marx attached considerable significance to Smith's confusion of value and revenue.

> But it is this category of 'revenue' which is to blame for all the harmful confusion in Adam Smith. The various kinds of revenue form with him the 'component parts' of the annually produced, newly created commodity-value, while vice versa, the two parts into which this commodity value resolves itself for the capitalist — the equivalent of his variable capital advanced in the form of money when purchasing labour, and the other portion of the value, the surplus-value, which likewise belongs to him but did not cost him anything — form sources of revenue. (II: 382)

And further:

> After starting by correctly defining the component parts of the value of the commodities and the sum of the value-product incorporated in them, and then demonstrating how these component parts form so many different sources of revenue, after thus deriving revenues from value, he proceeds in the opposite direction — and this remains his predominant conception — and turns the revenues into 'component parts' into 'original sources of all exchangeable value,' thereby throwing the doors wide open to vulgar economy. (II: 372)

Again insisting that we must start from capital if we are to grasp the concept of revenue and determine its size, Marx says:

> If I define the length of three straight lines independently and then

make these lines 'components' of a fourth straight line equal in length to their sum, this is no way the same procedure as if I start with a given straight line and divide this for some purpose or other — 'resolve' it so to speak — into three parts. The length of the line in the first case invariably changes with the length of the three lines whose sum it forms; in the latter case the length of the three segments is limited from the beginning by their forming parts of a line of given size. (ibid.: 383)

Keynes' Key Concepts

We have suggested that the departure points for the theoretical work of Marx and Keynes are of a diametrically opposed character: Marx insists that the crucial starting point for the examination of capitalism is the movement of capital, a movement which alone ultimately explains the nature and size of the various revenues or incomes in capitalist society. Keynes on the other hand starts his analysis from precisely this latter point, from income, or, to use his term, effective demand.

Keynes was concerned with one fundamental problem: the forms which determined the levels of investment and consumption. Now in the first place it is clear that these categories are not in any way unique or specific to capitalism. The consumption of wealth (as food, clothing, shelter) constitutes the material basis for life in all societies, whatever the specific conditions under which that wealth is produced and distributed. Similarly investment — the deployment of a portion of the current social wealth as a means of producing wealth in the future — is by no means an activity unique to capitalism but is present in all economies save the most primitive, where the low level of technique precludes the production of an economic surplus, at least on a regular and systematic basis. What we need to know is the specific form taken by that surplus and the manner in which it is extracted from those who produce it. Keynes here provides no answer for the simple reason that such questions do not enter his horizon.

In this connection, many writers have drawn attention to a striking fact about Keynes' entire orientation: namely, that the aggregates of his system are not centrally concerned with the specific form taken by consumption and investment within capitalist economy. Thus one writer has said,

One of the significant differences in the methodological character of the aggregate between Marx and Keynes lies in the direction in which abstraction is carried out. Marx's intention was to represent, as simply as possible, the specific interrelation of aggregates which is characteristic of capitalism, whereas Keynesian aggregates do not necessarily concern themselves with the specifics of capitalism. They are designed primarily to assist in accounting for the total level of employment under the simple assumption that it is proportional to the net national product. (Tsuru 1968)

Marx does not commence his analysis from the standpoint of national income and its division but with the total social capital and its basic disaggregation into constant capital (equivalent to expenditure on machinery, raw materials), variable capital (equivalent to the wages bill) and surplus value (in the form of profit, rent and interest).[7] Not only are these categories specific to capitalism but the contradictions which emerge between them are, according to Marx, an expression of an historically limited mode of production, capitalism. By comparison, the key concepts of *The General Theory* are abstract in the specific sense that they do not relate to the capitalist economic system as such. Keynes' theory is based on the proposition that three variables, the propensity to consume (consumption function), the inducement to invest (the marginal efficiency of capital) and the rate of interest (liquidity preference), in their interaction, determine the limits within which the national income fluctuates.

To take first the rate of interest: for Keynes this is determined by the quantity of money and 'liquidity preference'. (Liquidity preference Keynes defines as the 'natural' tendency of people to hold on to liquid assets in the absence of sufficient inducement — in the shape of interest — to relinquish this liquidity.) To understand the nature of liquidity preference it is necessary to know something of the 'psychological time preference' inherent in the propensity to consume. According to Keynes, each individual is confronted with two sets of time preferences on which he is obliged to act. First, the individual makes a decision about the proportion of his income to be spent now, and the proportion to be saved for future spending. Having decided the proportion to be saved, he must make a second decision: In what form are these savings to be held? As we know, Keynes proposed that there were three basic reasons for holding money, the speculative motive (the ability to take advantage of anticipated changes in prices) being the decisive one.

The rate of interest is the 'reward for parting with liquidity for a specified period', and is determined at the point where the desire to hold a certain amount of cash is just counterbalanced by the pull of the interest rate offered for that quantity of cash. Thus, as Keynes says, the interest rate is a 'highly psychological phenomenon' (GT: 202). It is not a payment for waiting or for abstinence as with pre-Keynesian economics, but for not hoarding (GT: 182), for parting with liquidity. Perhaps because Keynes became somewhat obsessed with the parasitic 'functionless investor', his theory ignores the fact that interest represents a return on money capital which is of the same general nature and origin as the return on all capital — in short, that interest is a segment of surplus value. Keynes' theory, which proposes that interest is formed from forces quite independent of the production process, singularly fails to grasp this essential point. This is hardly surprising given that interest-bearing capital, where money seems to breed money, appears *prima facie* to be quite separate from the production process. As Marx puts it, 'Capital appears as a mysterious and self-creating source of interest, a thing creating itself. . . . The use-value of money . . . becomes a faculty of money to generate money and yield interest just as it is the faculty of pear trees to bear pears' (III: 287).

But economics did not always hold to the sort of fetishistic view of interest as proposed by Keynes. Adam Smith, for instance, says:

> It may be laid down as a maxim, that whenever a great deal can be made by the use of money, a great deal will be given for the use of it; and that wherever little can be made by it, less will commonly be given for it. . . . The progress of interest, therefore may lead us to form some notion of the progress of profit. (Smith 1976: 105–6)

Interest, Smith implies, is merely part of the profit paid by the industrial capitalist to the money capitalist. Its limits are, therefore, fixed by the magnitude of profit. 'In any event, the average rate of profit is to be regarded as the ultimate determinant of the maximum rate of interest' (III: 353). This position of Marx was also held by the best of the classical school for 'according to the Ricardians and all other economists worth naming, the rate of interest is determined by the rate of profit' (Th I: 92).

It is for this reason, because profit and interest are both forms of one and the same category, namely surplus value, that they normally move together in the same direction. The demand for liquidity only becomes a potent force in periods of acute economic crisis. The fact that the owners of capital as a whole wish suddenly to transform their capital from its commodity into its money form is itself a graphic expression of a serious rupture in the turnover of capital. According to Keynes' liquidity preference theory, money assumes the form of a hoard and interest is the reward for not hoarding. In point of fact, however, the function of money as a hoard is but one of its several functions and all of them must be studied in their contradictory unity before we can group the real role of money within the capitalist economy.[8] For instance, one function of money, as everybody recognises, is as a means of payment. But this is a contradictory function, a fact by no means universally recognised. For when payments balance each other, money functions only nominally, as money of account, as measure of value. But when actual payments must be made, money no longer acts as a mere intermediary in the process of social metabolism but as the incarnation of wealth in the abstract, as the universal commodity. When, for whatever reason, there is a generalised disturbance in the developed system of payments, money ceases to play its hitherto merely nominal role as unit of account but now becomes the embodiment of social wealth as such. Previously the owners of capital had declared money to be an imaginary creation, and only commodities to constitute real value. Now, in times of sharp crisis, a different cry is heard and 'as the hart pants after fresh water, so pants the soul after money, the only wealth' (I: 266). It is thus in times of crises that the demand for money rises sharply and along with it the rate of interest which may now move quite out of line with the rate of profit. Thus, 'If we observe the cycles in which modern industry moves . . . we shall find that a low rate of interest generally corresponds to periods of prosperity, and a maximum of interest, up to the point of extreme usury corresponds to the period of crisis' (III: 353). And a little later Marx says,

> The rate of interest reaches its peak during crises, when money is borrowed at any cost to meet payments. Since a rise in interest implies a fall in the price of securities, this simultaneously opens a fine opportunity to people with available money-capital, to acquire at ridiculously low prices such interest-bearing securities as must, in the course of things, at least regain their average prices as soon as the rate of interest falls again. (III: 354)

In other words, it is in a crisis, when the rate of profit collapses, that the rate of interest may rise by leaps. It is under conditions of crisis that the rush for liquidity to meet obligations contracted during the phase of prosperity may become a controlling factor. As the pressure for liquidity becomes more generalised, a money famine may occur and bring about a sharp increase in interest rates as the price of other assets falls equally sharply. Many obligations cannot be met and a spate of bankruptcies ensues. It is under these conditions that the demand for liquidity for immediate means of payment becomes so pronounced that to the theoretically untrained eye it may seem to assume an entirely independent existence, such that it can be elevated into the determining cause of the crisis and not seen for what it is, as one of the symptoms of the crisis itself.

The last passage quoted from Marx is interesting in that it suggests that a theory of interest of the type proposed by Keynes took certain phenomena which emerge under conditions of crisis — when, by definition, all monetary and credit relations become violently disrupted — and generalised them into universal principles. As we have already pointed out, for Marx, interest is a return to money capital. It is, from this standpoint, of the same fundamental nature as the return on capital as a whole — it is the payment made out of surplus value earned on the entire capital for the use of a particular portion of that capital. Loan capital depends for its reward on its being successfully employed in the sphere of production. Thus Marx says, 'Loaning money as capital — its alienation on condition of its being returned after a certain time — presupposes, therefore, that it will be actually employed as capital, and that it actually flows back to its starting point' (III: 349). One entrepreneur (involved, let us suppose, in vehicle production) shares his total profit with another owner of capital (a banker, let us say) in return for a loan which is to be used with the aim of expanding his capital and surplus value. Returning to the most general form of capital, depicted by the circuit M–C–C'–M', an entrepreneur wishing to expand his capital must be prepared to do several things. First, he must part with his money capital, M. He must turn it into capital having a different form, C, by transforming it into labour power, materials and production equipment. Our entrepreneur must then put these various commodities through a process of production which will turn them into different commodities, C' which can (hopefully) be sold for an equivalent sum of money, M'. Thus has M been 'metamorphosised' as Marx puts it.

Now this initial parting with liquidity occurs quite independently of the proclivities of the owner of capital. Only on condition that capital is initially transformed from M into C can it continue to exist. Marx took great care to stress that in this process capital should not be viewed one-sidedly, as either M or C: it was in point of fact the unity of both these forms, forms which continually passed into each other. Capital was 'value in motion'. The process of capital accumulation arises not from the inclinations or preferences of the owner of capital: its imperatives stem from the very nature of capital itself and it is precisely because of this that the laws of its accumulation impose themselves upon the individual capitalist, indeed upon the owners of capital as a whole.

On this point, Keynes takes a radically different view. For according to him, the willingness of the owner of money to part with it is at root a psychological matter, not a reflection of the intrinsic needs of capital itself. Here Keynes is quite wrong in that money is always thrown into circulation on definite conditions, ones which are in the final analysis rooted in the realisation of a definite rate of profit. Should such conditions not be met, should there be a sudden collapse in the profit rate, then not only will money capital cease to be committed to circulation but as we have already suggested, the exact opposite can well occur: there will be a general rush for liquidity which will serve both to aggravate the crisis and to force up the rate of interest. (Naturally, miscalculations can be made by the owners of capital as to future profit prospects and under the appropriate circumstances this can clearly aggravate the problems of capital as a whole. But such miscalculations cannot, of themselves, form the basis for an explanation of a crisis.)

In the Keynesian scheme of things the rate of interest and the money supply are abstracted from the process of capital turnover; that is, from the very process in which they alone originate. Keynes' standpoint is that of the isolated individual who, given certain dispositions, makes a series of decisions about how to hold his wealth. There is here no concrete analysis of how money functions specifically within the capitalist system, and this notwithstanding the fact that Keynes rejected the idea present in some versions of neoclassicism that money was merely a veil, having no independent role. For the money from which the turnover of capital commences in the schema $M-C-C'-M'$ is not money merely but money functioning as capital — in short, money capital. In other words it can be understood only from the point of view of a worked-out scientific conception of capital and it is just this which is lacking in Keynes. Further, the existence of money playing the role not of money but of capital obviously implies the existence of capitalism but also capitalism at a point in its evolution where a differentiation between the various forms of capital has occurred — industrial capital, money capital, commodity capital, etc. If these specific relations are kept in view then the question of liquidity and the rate of interest will be approached in a manner quite different from that of Keynes. Whereas for Keynes the decision whether to hold one's assets in liquid form depends on expectations about future price movements and the rate of interest, for Marx the investigation of whether the owner of money capital will actually commit such capital to production depends upon the prevailing conditions of production, and critically upon the conditions under which surplus value is being extracted.

A final point in connection with the Keynesian theory of the rate of interest can be made. As we have already noted, for Keynes the rate of

interest is determined by the psychology of creditors and by the lending
policy of the banking system. To take this second factor, the amount of
money in circulation. Here Keynes' theory is deceptive, confusing as it
does the quantity of money and the amount of loan capital. But these
two are by no means the same thing ('The mass of loan capital is quite
different from the quantity of circulation' — III: 499). The former functions as capital, as a necessary initial phase in the circuit of capital. In
the event of inflation, given a growth of paper money in excess of the
requirements of commodity turnover and prices, an increase in the supply
of loan capital which will occur as a result of a growth of temporarily
free funds in the bank, will be counteracted by a depreciation of loan
capital resulting from inflation. Consequently, in these circumstances there
might be no increase in the real supply of loan capital. Here again is
revealed the fact that the phenomena of capitalism cannot be judged on
the basis of their immediate appearances but require real theoretical
analysis if they are to be grasped.

Keynes and the Falling Rate of Profit

In Marx's opinion, the tendency of the rate of profit to fall — a much
discussed and disputed question amongst the classical economists — was
the single most important law of political economy. This was so because
it was understood that it was the rate of profit which effectively regulated
the process of capital accumulation. In other words, profit was important not merely as one of several forms of income within the capitalist
system but as the source from which the means for the further accumulation of capital could alone come. In commenting on Ricardo, Marx
demonstrates the central importance which he attaches to the profit rate
and its tendency to decline, a tendency which Ricardo had himself sensed, if not fully grasped:

> The rate of profit is the compelling power of capitalist production,
> and only such things are produced as yield a profit. Hence the fright
> of the English economists over the decline in the rate of profit. That
> the bare possibility of such a thing should worry Ricardo, shows his
> profound understanding of the conditions of capitalist production . . .
> what worries Ricardo is the fact that the fundamental premise and driv-
> ing force of accumulation should be endangered by the development
> of production (III: 254)

The issue is also important in a consideration of the relationship between the economic theory of Keynes and that of Marx in so far as many writers have in the past likened Keynes' declining marginal efficiency of capital to Marx's theory of the tendency of the rate of profit to fall.[9]

Before dealing with Keynes' treatment of this matter, we can briefly set out, in somewhat formal terms, Marx's general notion of the falling rate of profit. Marx divides the total social capital into three broad categories: (1) constant capital (c), equivalent to expenditure on machinery, raw materials and heat, light and power. This capital was deemed constant in that it merely transfers the value embodied in it and cannot be the source of new value. (2) variable capital (v), the expenditure by capital on the purchase of labour power, variable because it is the only source for the expansion of value. (3) surplus value (s), the increment in value accruing to the owners of capital. The rate of profit is given by surplus value over total capital: $s/c + v$. Now as capital accumulates, there is a tendency for the constant capital to grow more rapidly than the variable portion of capital: this is the expression in value terms of the improvements in technology associated with capitalism throughout its history. The relatively rapid increase in constant capital as compared with the variable element of capital Marx refers to as the tendency for the organic composition of capital (c/v) to rise. Although an increase in the organic composition of capital will normally produce an increase in the rate of surplus value (s/v), or at least its mass (s), there are definite objective limits to such an increase, not least amongst them the actual physical limit to available working-time. But unless s/v does rise with sufficient rapidity to compensate for the increasing organic composition (c/v), then the tendency for the rate of profit to fall will assert itself in an actual fall.

This is the simplest possible outline of what is in reality a complex law, an outline which ignores both those many counteracting forces to its operation to which Marx drew attention, as well as to the long-standing disputes amongst Marxists about its proper interpretation. But the point to be stressed here is that, as far as Marx is concerned, the tendency for the rate of profit to decline was a product of forces intrinsic to capital. The essential quality of capital is that it is driven to expand and one result of this was the tendency for the rate of profit to fall. Now Keynes, no doubt in an effort to sharpen the impact of his own work, tried to create the impression that all orthodox writers throughout the nineteenth century had subscribed to the notion of a crisis-free capitalism. This was far from being the case; but what did characterise virtually all discussions of the problems associated with capital accumulation was that they were almost invariably seen as being located in disturbances emanating outside the actual social relations of capitalism. (Such was the case with Jevons' celebrated 'sunspot' theory of the trade cycle.)

Bearing this point in mind, we can consider Keynes' treatment of the movement of the marginal efficiency of capital. By capital Keynes means a thing, a 'capital asset' that yields an income. In interpreting capital as a series of assets that produce income, Keynes distinguishes two of its principal forms: 'instrumental capital' (a materialised form of capital engaged in the process of production, as in the case of a machine) and 'consumption capital' (a material form of capital operating in the sphere of consumption, like, for example, a house) (GT: 226). If we apply this definition to production, it would mean that by capital we have only means of production, that is, employing Marx's term, constant capital, and not the whole of capital which comprises both constant and variable elements. But in any event, the train of Keynes' overall argument indicates that by capital he means only its materialised elements, that is the means of production (a view shared by his radical followers, notably Joan Robinson). So it turns out that the marginal efficiency of capital is not to be equated with the Marxian rate of profit, as many appeared in the past to have assumed, since here profit is taken only in connection with constant capital rather than with the whole of capital.

According to Keynes' theory, any investment which is as yet unutilised will be carried out on one condition, that the anticipated rate of return over the cost of investment exceeds the rate of interest. Given that entrepreneurs aim at profit-maximisation, new investment will be carried on to the point at which the marginal efficiency of capital is equal to the interest rate. The marginal efficiency is determined by two factors: (a) the expected return from an income-yielding asset, and (b) the supply price, or replacement cost of the asset which is the source of that prospective yield. Such a yield takes the form of a flow of income over a period of time, a series of annuities over the anticipated life of the investment; if this stream of yields is then compared with the cost of supplying the assets necessary to produce these yields we have the marginal efficiency of capital, defined by Keynes thus:

> More precisely, I define the marginal efficiency of capital as being equal to the rate of discount which would make the present value of the series of annuities given by the returns expected from the capital-asset during its life just equal to the supply price. (GT: 135)

The prospective yields on an asset are undoubtedly for Keynes the key element in determining the marginal efficiency of capital. They are prospective rather than actual because at the moment the investment takes place they are nothing but expectations on the part of the investor. Because of the nature of capital assets, especially those of a long-term durable type, large immediate outlays are required before any returns are available to the investor. In Keynes' view capital assets are a link between the known present and an uncertain future.

Now why should the marginal efficiency of capital decline in the long run? Because, ran Keynes' argument, as more capital is invested it becomes more abundant (less scarce) and therefore produces a lower yield. Subscribing to the scarcity theory of capital, Keynes argues that the returns from capital assets exceed their supply price only because they are scarce (GT: 213). Every increase in investment brings an increase in output which competes with the output of existing capital. The growing volume of output tends to lower prices and hence to lower too the expected yields from future plant capacity. Keynes of course argued that if the interest rate was kept below the (declining) marginal efficiency of capital schedule then investment could continue unchecked. With ongoing investment, capital would at a certain point cease to be scarce and its return, or marginal efficiency, would then be reduced to zero, a prospect which might be realised within the space of one generation, Keynes felt. (Quite how capitalism could function with a zero rate of return to capital can only remain a sheer mystery from the point of view of the Marxist understanding of such a system. Keynes was in effect proposing the existence of capital without the existence of profit, not a very tolerable state of affairs for the owners of capital one might think!)

A familiarity with the history of economic theory reveals that in Keynes' explanation for a secular decline in the marginal efficiency of capital is to be found more than an echo of Adam Smith's theory of the falling rate of profit advanced some 150 years earlier. For it was Smith, following David Hume on this point, who sought to explain the decline in the rate of profit as a result of increasing competition amongst cápitals consequent upon accumulation. In *The Wealth of Nations* Smith says:

> The increase of stock, which raises wages, tends to lower profit. When the stocks of many rich merchants are turned into the same trade, their mutual competition naturally tends to lower its profit; and when there is a like increase of stock in all the different trades carried on in the same society, the same competition must produce the same effect in them all. (Smith 1976: 105)

And speaking of the decline of profits in the towns, Smith says

The stock accumulated in them comes in time to be so great, that it can no longer be employed with the ancient profit in that species of industry which is peculiar to them. That industry has its limits like every other; and the increase of stock, by increasing the competition, necessarily reduces the profit. (ibid.: 144–5)

Marx rejected such explanations for the decline in the rate of profit which were centred on competition. We can assume that the 'forces of competition' fix the rate of profit at 15 per cent, but the question still remains: Why is this figure 15 per cent? Why not 150 per cent? To ascribe the determination of the rate of profit to competition was, Marx held, to indulge in supply and demand explanations which left unexplored those forces which lay behind supply and demand. It led to a circular argument: the 'forces of competition' determined the rate of profit while at the same time the intensity of this competition was measured by precisely the self-same rate of profit. Naturally nobody denies the palpable fact of competition between capitals; Marx's point however was that this competition is merely the external, outer form in which the inner contradictions of capital expressed themselves. Competition is the realm in which the laws of capital are executed, but such laws are not *generated* in this sphere.

Keynes' explanation of the decline in the rate of profit, despite the fact that it is decked out in what superficially appears to be a new terminology, in the last resort rested upon the old neoclassical law of diminishing returns. Marx poured scorn on this 'law', first formulated in a clear manner by the eighteenth-century economist, Turgot, as being nothing more than a tautology, based on static assumptions, and in this respect little different from the Malthusian 'theory' of population which was also implicitly founded on the assumption of a static technology.

Keynes' theory of the marginal efficiency of capital was a law which purported to deal with a fundamental secular trend in capitalist economy, an economy characterised by just those forces from which the law abstracts, namely a tendency constantly to revolutionise the techniques of production. It is for this reason that Keynes has been attacked on the lack of realism attaching to this aspect of his theory, a criticism by no means confined to those sympathetic to Marxism. As Schumpeter (1952: 283), for instance, rightly pointed out about Keynes' theoretical devices: 'All the phenomena incident to the creation and change in this apparatus [industry], that is to say, the phenomena that dominate the capitalist process, are thus excluded from consideration.'

This quite artificial assumption of a 'given' technology has direct consequences for the Keynesian multiplier theory. This theory deals with the fact that consumption grows as a result of the expansion of production. The growth of Department I production (that producing means of production) actually creates an additional demand for machinery, raw materials, etc. as well as for the means of consumption of workers employed in this department. This in turn implies a growth of output in the other department — Department II, producing means of consumption. But the more rapid growth of the production of means of production signifies the growth of the productive power of social labour and is merely another way of expressing the fact that the organic composition of capital (the ratio of constant to variable capital) is increasing. An increase in the organic composition of capital finds expression in the relative, and in certain cases the absolute, decline in the demand for labour power. The accumulation of capital means the expansion of production on a new, higher level of technology. And this growth in the relative weight of constant as against variable capital will take place in both departments of the economy. The results of this increase in the organic composition depend upon the precise nature of the rise, but one thing does follow: although the accumulation of capital (for the Keynesian, an increase in investment) may bring about an absolute increase in the numbers employed, it will cause a relative lowering of employment. Consequently there is no precise relationship between an increase in investment and an increase in employment; although it might be possible to obtain such a relationship for previous investment, it is one disrupted every time new investment takes place in so far as such investment almost invariably takes place at a new, higher level of productive technique. So here again Keynesianism abstracts from the features specific to capitalism, namely that the development of the productive forces takes the form of a rising organic composition of capital and that production does, in the final analysis, depend on the level of consumption.

There is one final consequence of Keynes' assumption of a given technology which is worthy of note: namely, that it cannot offer any adequate explanation for the cyclical movement of the rate of profit. If, as capital accumulates and it becomes 'less scarce' such that its marginal efficiency declines, then the rate of profit can move in one direction only: downwards. It implies that the fundamental problem of capitalism is one not of the cyclical alteration of booms and slumps but of stagnation and steady decline, as we have noted, precisely the direction in which a number of Keynes' followers, such as Alvin Hansen in the United States, did indeed interpret his work. Here again it must be emphasised that Marx's view was of a quite different order. For despite interpretations to the contrary, there is no element of mechanicalism in his conception of the tendency of the rate of profit to fall. Precisely because this law reflected the clash of both objective and subjective factors (which latter included the strength of the working class, its degree of consciousness, the quality of its leadership, etc.), its empirical unfolding could never be known in advance. Capital makes continual efforts to overcome the effects of the operation of this law, but in so doing only raises ever greater obstacles to the smooth, crisis-free expansion of the productive forces: such is the contradictory nature of the capitalist system: 'Capitalist production is continually engaged in the task of overcoming these imminent barriers, but it overcomes them only by means which place the same barriers in its way in a more formidable size' (III: 243).

Keynes on Consumption

We can consider briefly the final component of Keynes' system, namely consumption. Here again the overall tendency of his work, to abstract from the social relations specific to capitalism, is all too evident. (It is noteworthy that orthodoxy on the whole deals with 'the consumer' as one of the central actors, if not the central actor, on the economic stage. Naturally, such a person is an empty abstraction, torn from all social and class relations. The fact that 'everybody is a consumer' is a proposition which serves to hide the antagonistic divisions which characterise capitalist society.)

Keynes' propositions about consumption have already been mentioned, are well known, and thus require no more than a brief outline. First, he held that because of the existence of the marginal propensity to consume — according to Keynes a fundamental psychological law — the gap between income and consumption would grow, and unless this gap was appropriately bridged the level of income would fall below that needed to sustain full employment. Various measures were available to raise the level of income including a certain degree of income redistribution, although Keynes was careful to insist that this should be of only 'moderately conservative' proportions.

For Keynes 'consumption' is the consumption of all individuals in society, each individual being subject to the basic psychological law which he believed determined the relationship between income and consumption. This is far from being Marx's approach. He drew a distinction between individual consumption on the one hand and industrial consumption on the other. An analogous distinction is that between buyer and consumer. The buyer for Marx is someone who uses up something for his own needs whereas the act of consumption involves using up something in the process of labour. The purchases carried out by the majority of the population within capitalist economy excludes the greater part of the commodities produced in such an economy. For workers buy no instruments of labour, no raw materials; they buy only articles of subsistence, that is, commodities which enter into individual as opposed to 'productive' consumption. Marx explains the significance of this point when he says:

> This also shows the ambiguity of the word consumer and how wrong it is to identify it with the word buyer. As regards industrial consumption, it is precisely the workers who consume machinery and raw materials, using them up in the labour process. But they do not use them up for themselves and they are therefore not buyers of them. Machinery and raw materials are for them neither use-values nor commodities, but objective conditions of a process of which they themselves are the subjective conditions. (Th II: 518)

Marx is here in effect insisting that it is not possible to deal with the level of consumption in the abstract, a-socially, explaining it by reference to a supposed universal psychological disposition on the part of each separate individual. Within the capitalist system consumption takes place always within definite economic (class) relations and it is only by starting with these quite objective relations that the real nature of consumption and its limits can be analysed. As far as the capitalist system is concerned the essential features of these economic relations, as they affect consumption, are (1) the majority of the producers (the working class) are non-consumers (non-buyers in Marx' terminology) of the greater part of their products, namely the means of production and raw materials, and (2) the majority of producers can consume the equivalent of their product on one condition: that they create surplus value. In short, the level of consumption of the working class cannot be deemed to be determined by the psychological proclivities of a large number of disparate individuals, but by the amount of variable capital (the equivalent to the wage bill) which in turn depends upon the rate of capital accumulation. If this is so then we have but a further illustration of the fact that it is impossible to understand any aspect of capitalist economy unless one starts from the nature of capital and its turnover.

Once Again on the Nature of Capital: The Case of Joan Robinson

We have deliberately concentrated on the conflicting conceptions of capital in the work of Marx and Keynes. This we have done, given that the problem of the essence of capital affects the innermost nature of the production of wealth in contemporary society. We have suggested that Keynes' treatment of capital is amongst other things characterised by a desire to divorce it from its real relation to production: 'It is much preferable to speak of capital as having a yield over the course of its life in excess of its original cost, than as being productive' (GT: 213). So says Keynes, thus in effect reducing the matter to one of semantics only. His sole concern is not with the source of the 'yield from capital' but the grounds on which an asset as capital brings a yield in excess of its 'supply price'. As we know he finds these grounds in the scarcity of such assets.

This chapter has spoken of the decisive importance for Marxists of a theoretically sound critique of Keynes, given the efforts of a number of writers to construct a bridge between Marx and Keynes (albeit a suitably interpreted Keynes). Joan Robinson has here been the decisive figure for such attempts. It goes without saying that Robinson for long occupied a central position in the economic theory of the twentieth century. A member of the famous 'Cambridge Circus' which helped Keynes formulate the ideas which produced *The General Theory*, she has been a leading defender of the Keynes tradition in the years after his death, against both his 'friends' as well as his declared enemies. No Marxist, she has nevertheless always claimed considerable sympathy for the ideas of Marx. Politically, throughout the post-war years she identified herself with a number of radical causes. Given these several facets to her work, her views are of considerable interest in the context of the issues raised in this chapter. She has of course also been in the vanguard of those criticising some of the cherished propositions of neoclassical economics, particularly those which deal with the alleged 'productivity' of capital. We have not been concerned here with the nature of these criticisms as such. They stem essentially from the work of Sraffa, first begun in the 1920s. The Cambridge school has persistently drawn attention to those problems which orthodox neoclassical theory has encountered in connection with the theory of capital. They can be summarised as follows. This theory contains no prerequisites for aggregating capital goods, that is for discovering the true basis that unites things to form capital and determine its size. Second, in any theory linking the origin and returns on capital with the matter of time a vicious circle ensues: the size of capital is determined by capitalising future revenues, but to establish this method a rate of interest is required; this is however a magnitude the size of which depends upon the amount of capital. This is the nub of the criticisms of orthodox theory made by those in the Sraffa school. (For Marxists it can be said that these problems are the reflection of a decisive confusion, one involving the lumping together of the socio-historical substance of capital with its material form, and in particular one that entails the confusion of 'capital' with 'means of production'. This confusion persists throughout Keynes' work.)

Now the question is: Has the Cambridge school really got to the bottom of the issue in their criticisms of the neoclassical notion of capital? Joan Robinson outlines her idea of the problem of the productivity of capital when she says:

> Whether we choose to say that capital is productive or that capital is necessary to make labour productive, is not a matter of much importance [here, as with Keynes, the matter is reduced to that of a purely semantic problem]. . . . Indeed, a langauge that compels us to say that capital (as opposed to the ownership of capital) is not productive rather obscures the issue. It is more cogent to say that capital, and the application of science to industry, are immensely productive, and that the institutions of private property, developing into monopoly, are deleterious because they prevent us from having as much capital, and the kind of capital, that we need. (Robinson 1941: 18)

Now, unless one takes the view that, like value, capital is 'just a name' the issue as to whether capital is productive, and if so in what precise sense, is by no means a matter of word definitions, but a central, indeed the central question for economic theory. This is demonstrated by amongst other things the history of economics, which has been forced continually to grapple with the mystery presented by capital.[10]

It follows from the standpoint of Marx's theory of capitalism that only labour (more precisely abstract labour) creates value. But it is by no means a consequence of this view that in the opinion of Marxism the 'objective factors of production' (machines, etc.) are to be denied any form of 'productivity', as Robinson suggests ('Thus Marx's refusal to treat capital as a factor of production seems well founded' (1975: 19)) Quite the opposite is the case: to the extent that such factors raise the level of labour productivity they most certainly contribute to the production of wealth, that is to use values. The word 'productivity' however here carries two distinct meanings. First, it can be used to denote the production of use values; it can also indicate that definite social relations are being produced and reproduced. When Marx stressed that capital is productive he did so from a definite angle: as the predominant social relation of capitalist society. And its productivity is from this standpoint quite specific: it is productive of surplus labour which takes the form of interest, profit, etc. And capital was in a position to extract such labour not at all because it involved 'waiting', because 'risk' was involved, was 'scarce', functioned as a 'means of production' or furthered the 'application of science to industry' (Robinson). Capital is productive precisely because it was an essential historical relation for the extraction of surplus labour and far more 'productive' in this sense than was feudalism or any other pre-capitalist form of economy. A steam engine in a mine is productive of use values (or rather the labour materialised in such an engine is productive) but this has nothing whatsoever to do with its being capital. It would be equally productive of wealth were it owned by the workers at the mine rather than the entrepreneur. We are dealing here not at all with a matter of words but with a central question: Do we derive the meaning of the word productivity from the relations of man to nature or from the relations of man to man? In other words is there a distinction to be made between productivity in the abstract and something which is productive specifically for capital? In Marx's opinion not only is there a distinction here but a profound and ever-deepening contradiction: that which is productive for human beings (particularly the working class and other oppressed people) is increasingly positively unproductive (unprofitable) for capital.[11] (Robinson's distinction between capital and the ownership of capital confuses precisely the essence of the matter: that capital being a social relation cannot exist apart from definite relationships of ownership. Like those utopian socialists of the nineteenth century criticised by Marx, she wants to get rid of the capitalists while retaining capital. But of course to eliminate the one is necessarily to eliminate the other.) When Keynes advanced his scarcity theory of the return to capital he was clearly 'explaining' its productivity from the former point of view; that is, from the point of view of the relationship of man to nature: capital is productive because it exists in only limited quantity, just as land yields a rent because it is 'scarce'. And so with Robinson who conflates capital with 'the application of science to industry', a purely natural phenomena.

The Concept of Equilibrium

One persistent theme amongst many of the radical Keynesians is their hostility to the notion of equilibrium. Now one thing Marx and Keynes certainly shared in common was their rejection of Say's law, the notion that capitalism was an automatically self-equilibrating economic system. But their agreement on this point in fact hides more than it tells us because the grounds on which Marx opposed Say were fundamentally different from those of Keynes. We have suggested that in his characterisation of the development of nineteenth-century economic thought, Keynes attached far too much weight to Say's law of markets. Indeed, as we have noted, in his redefinition of classical economics, Keynes went so far as to make the acceptance of Say's law the distinguishing criterion for membership of that school, a solecism which enabled him to include not only Ricardo (for Marx the last of the classical economists) but all those who followed Ricardo down to and including Keynes' contemporary, Pigou.

There is no doubt that the widespread support given to Say's contention that disequilibrium within capitalist economy is in principle impossible was a significant expression of the increasingly apologetic nature of nineteenth-century economics, as well as a reflection on the part of sections of the middle class for social peace and stability. But it does not follow from this that the denial of any long-run disequilibrium within bourgeois economy marked the real essence of the vulgar school of which Say is the true father. Nor does it follow either that the rejection of the notion of equilibrium, after the fashion of post-Keynesianism, constitutes a sound basis either for the criticism of neoclassical economics or for the establishment of a theory which grasps the real movement of capitalism. We have argued that the degeneration of classical economics resided not in its acceptance of Say's law (Ricardo had, after all, accepted Say's proposition in opposition to Malthus[13]) but arose from a deeper, more universal source: in the conscious removal of a consideration of the social relations of production from the province of economics. It was this turn away from an analysis of the (antagonistic) relations of bourgeois economy, a justification of the capitalist system as one based on a natural and eternal harmony of interests, that transformed the science of political economy into the ideology of the vulgar school. In this respect Keynes was far from justified in lumping together Say and Ricardo on the grounds that they shared a common belief in the inherently stable nature of capitalist production, however convenient this device might have been for the pedagogic purposes of *The General Theory*.

We have attempted to demonstrate that at the level of his basic categories Keynes adopted the standpoint of the vulgar school which started its analysis not from the objective social relations of capitalist economy but from the immediate reflection of those laws in the consciousness of the participants in bourgeois production. Thus when Marx criticised Say's assertion that capitalism assured the conditions for equilibrium, and automatically so, Marx pointed out that Say was able to reach this (false) conclusion only by ignoring precisely those features which were specific to capitalism. Concretely, when Say proposed that 'supply creates its own demand' (Marx called this 'childish babbling' and 'unworthy' of Ricardo when he repeated it) he had in fact assumed the conditions not of capitalist production but of elementary barter. 'The conceptions adopted by Ricardo from the tedious Say, that overproduction is not possible, or at least that no general glut of the market is possible, is based on the proposition that products are exchanged against products' (Th II: 493).

Marx objected to Say's proposition — that supply and demand would always exist in a state of equilibrium — because it was an empty tautology, emptied, that is, of any social and historical content. Naturally the categories of supply and demand exist within capitalist economy, just as the categories which are the basis of Keynes' system (investment, consumption, savings, etc.) certainly exist in an empirical sense. But in order to analyse concretely supply and demand within such an economy one had to understand that the production of wealth takes on a specific social form — the production of commodities for the market, and that the supply and demand for commodities was shaped by the feature which dominates in this economy — its division into the two great classes, one which monopolises the means of production and another dependent entirely on the sale of its labour power. In connection with commodity production, a commodity, as something meeting a specific human need is a use value; but at the same time it has a definite exchange value, signifying the fact that it constituted a proportion of total social labour. Marx objected to Say's empty proposition because in effect it obscured the contradictory nature of all wealth produced within the capitalist economy.

The gist of Marx's argument on this point runs as follows. Let us take the case of a manufacturer supplying steel. He supplies in a given period of time an amount of steel of a definite use value; say 10 tons of the metal of a certain quality. At the same time he supplies steel of a specific exchange value, signified by its price, £500. But between these two sides of the commodity there is a profound difference which formal thought obscures. For on the one hand the manufacturer places steel with a definite use value on the market which, because of its physical characteristics, is capable of supplying definite needs. At the same time the exchange value of this steel exists only ideally in the shape of a price for the steel which has still to be realised. The seller of the steel is interested in one thing and one thing alone: the exchange value of his steel. He supplies a use value but he is concerned only with the exchange value he will thereby obtain (in money). It is, of course, quite possible for the exchange value of the steel to be expressed in quite different quantities of the metal and indeed this will be the case when there are changes in the productivity of labour in steel-making. The supply of the use value and the supply of the exchange value to be realised are thus by no means identical, since quite different quantities of use value can be represented in the same quantity of exchange value. And just because the exchange value of the steel supplied, but yet to be realised, and the quantity of steel do not coincide, there can be no grounds, *a priori*, for assuming that there will be no contradiction between these two polar opposites.

The point here is that Marx did not object to Say because he employed the notion of equilibrium as such but because in the proposition that supply and demand always necessarily balance the specific social relations lying behind these abstractions were not considered and nor therefore was the possibility of a contradiction arising between them. Say, in short, reached his conclusions on the basis of empty, purely formal abstractions.

It must never be forgotten, that in capitalist production what matters is not the immediate use-value but the exchange-value and, in particular, the expansion of surplus-value. This is the driving motive of capitalist production, and it is a pretty conception that — in order to reason away the contradictions of capitalist production — abstracts from its very basis and depicts it as a production aiming at the direct satisfaction of producers. (Th II: 495)

And further:

since the circulation process of capital is not completed in one day but extends over a fairly long period until the capital returns to its original form, since this period co-incides with the period within which market-prices equalise with cost prices, the great upheavals and changes take place in the productivity of labour and therefore also in the real value of commodities, it is quite clear, that between the starting-point, the prerequisite capital, and the time of its return at the end of one of these periods, great catastrophes must occur and elements of crisis must have gathered and develop, and these cannot in any way be dismissed by the pitiful proposition that products exchange for products. The comparison of value in one period with the value of the commodities in a later period is no scholastic illusion . . . but rather forms the fundamental principle of the circulation process of capital. (Th II: 493)

An analysis of capital must take not only the specific social relations of this mode of production into account but must grasp its movement as a whole — in all its interconnected and contradictory moments. The essence of eclecticism is to take bits and pieces from what is a unified process and combine them into a series of empty abstractions. However flexible this may appear to be, however seemingly 'undogmatic' such eclecticism seems to the untrained mind, Marx rightly insists upon a different method: in this instance one that aims to grasp capital as a whole in the course of its real development. And if this is the aim of science it becomes impossible to separate out the moments of equilibrium from those of disequilibrium in any absolute sense; this is so because the conditions for the equilibrium of bourgeois economy grow out of the conditions of its disequilibrium, and vice versa. Here the formal method of economics is quite lost. During the period of boom the vulgar eye is directed exclusively to those indices — production figures, growth of trade, expansion of investment — which mirror only the surface outward forms of the capitalist economy. Such empirical 'facts' can be compared in any number of ways, and many economists spend their time doing little but just this. In a slump all such indicators tend to be transformed into their opposite. Again, following the prescription of positivism, the indicators can once more be compared in an effort to explain the transformation. But because bourgeois economics does not penetrate beneath the surface of immediate economic 'data' (declaring such efforts to be impossible or to involve 'metaphysics') this transformation, while it may be recorded empirically, can never be understood theoretically. To understand any phenomena theoretically, scientific concepts are essential. And just because these are lacking in orthodox economics, neither the periods of upswing nor the periods of slump which grow organically out of boom conditions can ever be comprehended.[14]

Marx's analysis of the production of individual capitals could perhaps give rise to the false impression that the sole object of capitalist production — the creation of value and above all the creation of surplus value — is one in which the role of use values can be left out of account. When Marx comes to study the production and reproduction of social capital, that is capital considered as a whole, this is shown not to be the case, for it transpires that this production of value and surplus value is indeed constrained by a barrier which was not taken into consideration in the earlier analysis, namely the barrier constituted by use value on a social scale. In order to reproduce its capital, society must not only have a total fund of value available but it has to find these values ready to hand in a particular useful form; that is, in definite material shape (as machines, raw materials, means of subsistence, etc.). And all these various things must present themselves in proportions determined by the technical requirements of production, proportions which, because methods of production are undergoing continual change, must alter over time.

At the same time, however, Marx's basic proposition — that capitalism is a system founded on the production and reproduction of surplus value, and a process in which the satisfaction of human needs is an entirely incidental matter — still holds. That is to say, human needs are only met to the degree that satisfying them is a means to the accumulation of surplus value. It is this ever-present growing and developing contradiction between use value and exchange value which lies at the heart of the contradictions of capitalism.

Marx in no way denies the possibility of a solution to this contradiction. But it is the nature of this solution which must be carefully considered.[15] The 'Reproduction Schemes' of vol. II of *Capital* provide the key to grasping this contradiction and manner in which capitalism deals with it. Marx divides social production into two large departments, that producing means of consumption for both the basic classes (Department II), and that producing means of production out of which the existing stock of capital is replaced and extended (Department I). Marx shows how each department is obliged to work for the other, thus establishing a series of complex reciprocal relationships between them. Each department can replace its necessary elements of production only on condition that it obtains a fraction of these elements from the other department and in a suitable material form. On the other hand, each department only comes into possession of the use values it needs if it obtains them from the other department by means of the exchange of equivalent values. In these schemata of reproduction, Marx aims to establish not only the manner in which all the components of the annual value product of society $(c + v + s)$ mutually replace each other. For he also demonstrates how a proportion of the total surplus value produced can be devoted to the further expansion of capitalist production, which naturally presupposes the regular exchange of these value components and their realisation on the market. In this sense the schemes of reproduction in the *Capital* are an aspect of Marx's solution to the realisation problem.

It should be noted that this division of the capitalist economy into two basic sections was for Marx no arbitrary one. The product of Department I is, in physical terms, machinery and equipment, materials of various kinds such as fuel and electricity which are consumed productively. The products of Department II (food, clothing, housing) can only be used for personal, non-productive consumption. Marx's central aim, following the example of Quesnay, was to portray the many individual acts of circulation which appear on the surface of society in their characteristic movement, that is in the light of 'the circulation between the great functionally determined economic classes of society' (II: 363). Here Marx's distinction between productive consumption and personal consumption is of a quite different nature from the consumption/investment distinction of Keynes. Whereas Marx's analytical separation is in the last resort a reflection of the basic class division of society, that of Keynes is devoid of real social content in that for him the distinction between consumption and investment is confined essentially to the question of time.

As we have already indicated, a number of economists — James Mill, Ricardo and Say amongst them — in fact 'solved' this problem of the relationship of production to consumption, but only in a superficial manner. They did so by confusing capitalist production (M–C–M') with simple commodity production (C–M–C) and the latter with barter (C–C). Any act of production, according to this view, creates its own demand, and since, in the last analysis, products are by definition exchanged for products there is an automatic equilibrium of sellers and buyers. But it is a conclusion established not through an investigation of the actual processes of production and circulation in capitalist economy but one arrived at through arbitrary and quite unrealistic assumptions. If the assumptions proposed by Say are accepted the only source of capitalist breakdown will occur if, for whatever reasons, commodities are not produced in the right proportions. In other words, the crisis of capitalism would be one of disproportionality.

Sismondi took a diametrically opposed position on the question of equilibrium within the capitalist economy. Unlike the English classical economists he regarded the commodities appearing on the market not merely as the products of labour but as the products of capital. He believed that capital is able to generate an increase in value; that is, create the conditions for its own self-expansion, because the owner of capital does not pay the full production costs and essentially because he gives the worker an insufficient wage in return for his labour. For him it is precisely this increase in value which provides the source for the accumulation of capital. But then the question must arise: How can the surplus product be sold if the worker who has produced it cannot buy back the portion of the product corresponding to his labour, and if the capitalists themselves do not consume this surplus product (a proposition which follows if a part of it has been capitalised)? Sismondi regarded this as creating an insurmountable problem. He believed that in the final analysis the realisation of surplus product was impossible, unless, that is, it was disposed of, and thus realised, abroad.

Marx rejected both Malthus' and Sismondi's 'solutions' as being equally one-sided and therefore ultimately false. He did not wish to deny that the realisation of surplus value was a real problem for the capitalist economy. He did however reject Sismondi's doubts as to the possibility of realisation under capitalism. According to Marx, capitalist production does in fact create its own market and in this way it is able to 'solve' the problem of the realisation of surplus value. But it does so not in a metaphysical manner (by abolishing the problem) but in a truly dialectical sense. It solves it, that is to say, by raising this problem to an ever higher and wider — in short, more universal — level. Or, to be more concrete, the realisation problem is resolved only to the extent that the capitalist mode of production advances, only to the extent that it constantly expands its internal and external markets. In this regard, extended reproduction of capital is neither purely impossible, nor can it proceed for ever, uninterruptedly, without breaks, without discontinuities, as the classical economists imagined to be the case. Capitalism 'solves' the problem of realisation by taking its internal contradictions to an ever higher level, by continually producing and reproducing them on an ever wider basis until the point where they engulf the whole of society and create the possibilities for the transition to socialism.

For Marx, phases of expansion and of relative equilibrium lead inexorably to their opposites and it is through the form of crises that the contradictions accumulated during the phase of expansion are finally and violently resolved by means of a destruction of capital; this serves to bring the total social capital once more into an appropriate relationship with the total pool of surplus value. Speaking of the many influences which are at work during the period of expansion, Marx says:

> These different influences may at one and the same time operate predominantly side by side in space and time and at another succeed each other in time. From time to time the conflict of antagonistic agencies finds vent in a crisis. The crises are always but momentary and forcible solutions of the existing contradictions. They are violent

eruptions which for a time restore the disturbed equilibrium. (III: 244)

It is clear that Marx objected to the notion of equilibrium advanced by Say. But one should not conclude from this that such a concept has no place in his analysis. He certainly criticised Say and other economists for having abstracted the notion of equilibrium from the social relations which constitute the real foundation of capitalist economy. This allowed the apologists to make this category absolute. And they were thereby able to declare that equilibrium was a 'natural', 'normal' condition while movement away from it was but a temporary, passing aberration.

But, we stress, this should not lead us to the conclusion that Marx excludes the concept of equilibrium from his work. Let us consider this from the point of view of the law of value. If we assume that two products of labour exchange at their labour value we assume an equilibrium exists between the two given branches of production. Changes in the labour value of a product destroy this equilibrium and cause a transfer of labour from one branch of production to another, thereby bringing about consequent redistribution of the forces of production in the economy. It is changes in the productive powers of labour which cause changes in the amount of labour needed for the production of given commodities, setting in motion corresponding increases or decreases in the value of commodities.

The above mechanism Marx sees as an expression of the functioning of petty commodity production. Under the conditions of capitalist production the process through which equilibrium is simultaneously shattered and established is of a different, higher order. Under capitalism the organisation of production no longer resides in the hands of individual, petty producers, but is now organised by industrial capitalists. Capitalists invest their capital in the sphere of production which is most profitable. The transfer of capital to a given sphere of production creates increased demand for labour power in that particular branch of the economy. As a result, assuming other things to be equal, this brings about an increased price of labour power (wages). This draws living labour into this expanding sector. The distribution of the productive forces amongst the various spheres of the economy and the establishment of conditions of relative equilibrium between them takes the form of the distribution of capitals amongst them. It is the movement of capital, the decisive element of bourgeois production, which is the source of stabilisation and destabilisation alike. Wage labour must move in response to the needs of capital. In short, 'Wage labour subordinated by capital . . . must submit to being transferred in accordance with the requirements of capital and to be transferred from one sphere of production to another' (III). Specifically it is the movement of capital from those areas with low profit rates to those with higher rates which brings about a tendency towards equilibrium and the establishment of a general rate of profit.

But again this tendency must be seen as a process which is realised not in any mechanical manner. Like all laws it can never appear in unadulterated form. That is, it never produces a situation in which there is actually a general rate of profit throughout the economy. As in the case of all laws, we are faced with a tendency, a contradictory movement towards a never attainable equilibrium, and a movement which must take the form of necessary and constant disruptions. It is this contradictory movement Marx is speaking of when he refers to the 'incessant equilibrium of constant divergences' (III: 192).

Now the neo-Keynesians rightly object to the fact that orthodox neoclassical theory treats capitalist economy as though it were a machine, tending by its very nature towards equilibrium. This does not mean however that the whole notion of equilibrium should be consigned to the rubbish bin, as Kaldor and others tend to suggest.[16] The fact is that there is a certain tendency within capitalism towards equilibrium but this is a tendency not to be treated as absolute, nor as a state in which capitalism 'naturally' exists but as one attained through just that incessant equilibrium of constant divergences of which Marx speaks. If we consider the movement of the rate of profit and, we repeat, it is this movement which is most significant in the functioning and development of bourgeois economy, it is the existence of the tendency for the establishment of a general rate of profit which serves to pull supply and demand into balance, only to disrupt that equilibrium in the very course of its establishment. Those who see in capitalism only an equilibriating mechanism do of course take a one-sided (and usually an apologetic) view of the capitalist system. But equally one-sided are those who see capitalism as one based exclusively on disequilibrium.

The necessary laws of any series of phenomena find their way, establish themselves, through a maze of deviations. Superficially, such deviations appear as contingent occurrences; yet it is only though such apparent accidents that the law, necessity, establishes itself. At the same time, because it is in such deviations that the tendency is expressed, there are also introduced into the process many new aspects which do not flow from necessity but are conditioned by external circumstances. Take as an instance the Marxist law of value. This holds that there is a necessary relationship between the prices of commodities and their values — the amount of socially necessary labour for its production. This connection manifests itself, and can only manifest itself, in the shape of constant divergences of value from price, first in one direction and then another. Such deviations are, as already indicated, precisely the mechanism through which the general rate of profit is established under conditions where the organic composition of capital — the ratio of constant to variable capital — is not uniform throughout the various branches of the economy.

To underscore the point that Marx recognised that the concept of equilibrium was a necessary abstraction — that is to say, a necessary moment in the real path of capitalist development — we can refer to a passage in which he discusses the function of the general rate of profit. He starts by saying that if we assume that the forces of supply and demand are in equilibrium, we have then to explain the phenomena in which we are interested in this case price) by means of forces other than those of supply and demand:

> If supply equals demand, they cease to act, and for this very reason commodities are sold at their market-values. Whenever two forces operate equally in opposite directions, they balance one another, exert no outside influences, and any phenomena taking place within these circumstances must be explained by causes other than these two forces. If supply and demand balance one another they cease to explain anything, do not affect market values, and therefore leave us so much in the dark as to why the market value is expressed in just this sum of money and no other. (III: 186)

Marx then proceeds to explain why it is necessary to assume, for the purposes of analysis, that supply and demand coincide, even though in reality this is not the case. Such a procedure was necessary 'to be able to study phenomena in their fundamental relations, in the form corresponding to their conception, that is to study them independently of the appearances caused by the movement of supply and demand.' And there is an additional reason. This was to allow thought

> to find the actual tendencies of their movements and to some extent to record them. Since the inconsistencies are of an antagonistic nature, and since they continually succeed one another, they balance out one another through their opposing movement and their mutual contradiction. Since, therefore, supply and demand never equal one another in any given case, their differences follow one another in such a way — and the result of a deviation in one direction is that it calls forth a deviation in the opposite direction — that supply and demand are

always equated when the whole is viewed over a certain period, but only as an average of past movements, and only as the continuous movement of their contradiction. (III: 186).

In examining Keynes' basic theoretical conceptions we have argued that far from marking any advance on the work of his classical predecessors they constitute a serious degeneration, for whereas Smith, Ricardo and others set out to establish the objective laws of capitalism, Keynes' work is deeply imbued with the subjectivism which characterises bourgeois thought as a whole in the twentieth century. In the first place, as we have tried to show, his work was highly eclectic, drawing on elements from the neoclassical school for its explanation of the laws of distribution, yet at the same time calling on Malthus for the explanation of the poverty of the 1930s. It was for this reason, because Keynes' work resembled a rag-bag, that anybody could dip in and choose what they wanted. This is certainly connected with Keynes' view of the state as a supra-class institution, a point examined in the previous chapter. The state was an institution to be used to direct the economy according to one's ideas. But this must leave open the question of precisely which policies are to be pursued. Sismondi and Proudhon employed an analysis not unlike that of Keynes to advocate utopian socialist ideas; Malthus used his under-consumptionism to defend the position of feudalism within a rapidly advancing capitalism; in the twentieth century (under quite different historical conditions when capitalism had ceased to be a force for progress) both Fascism and social democracy have operated economic policies which can claim legitimate parentage in Keynes. That such conflicting ideologies are able to find some degree of support in Keynes' economic theory is no accident given that (a) it was confined to the sphere of circulation (taking the relations of production as given), and (b) it operated with subjective psychological categories.

Keynes' three independent variables (GT: 246–7) do not even mention profit which for Keynes took back-seat to the gambling instinct which was supposedly inherent in human nature, for 'If human nature felt no temptation to take a chance, no satisfaction (profit apart) in constructing a factory, a railway, a mine or a farm, there might not be much investment as a result of cold calculation' (GT: 150). And what are we to make of an economic theory, which after all claimed to explain some of the fundamental problems of twentieth-century capitalism, which could declare: 'In estimating the prospects of investment, we must have regard, therefore, to the nerves and hysteria and even the digestions and reactions to the weather of those upon whose spontaneous activity it largely depends' (ibid.: 162)?

Despite its obvious weaknesses, Keynesianism was certainly an important strand in post-war bourgeois ideology. It was the theory which legitimated government spending and the creation of the Welfare State. In the next chapter we shall examine the economic implications of such expenditures.

Notes

1. In the same book Kregal makes a similar point when he says: 'The Keynesian [theory], on the other hand, is more closely linked to Ricardo and Marx of the classical tradition, of the analysis of value in physical terms, the analysis of quantities in terms of some type of measure based on labour, and of the analysis of a system undergoing change through historical time' (1975: 33).

2. One issue involved in the critique of Baran and Sweezy is their notion of economic surplus. As part of their disposal of the categories of Marx they substitute the notion of economic surplus for that of surplus value. These terms are, of course, by no means the same; all societies, save the most primitive, generate an economic surplus. Only under capitalism does this surplus take the form of surplus value.

3. Keynes was certainly not as accommodating to Marx. He asserted that Marx's ideas were 'characterised . . . by mere logical fallacy', and he believed that 'Marxian Socialism must always remain a portent to the historians of opinion — how a doctrine so illogical and dull can have exercised so powerful and enduring an influence on the minds of men, and through them the events of history' (Keynes, *Laissez-Faire and Communism*, quoted in Hunt 1979: 377). Elsewhere Keynes could say, 'How can I adopt a creed which, preferring the mud to the fish, exalts the boorish proletariat above the bourgeoisie and intelligentsia who, with whatever faults, are the quality in life and carry the seeds of all human advancement?' (JMK: CEW 9). And this from a man who on the one hand had failed to make even a cursory inspection of Marx's ideas but nevertheless knew that his own work would destroy its foundations.

4. 'Once and for all may I state, that by classical Political Economy, I understand that economy which, since the time of W. Petty, has investigated the real relations of production in bourgeois society, in contradistinction to vulgar economy, which deals with appearances only, ruminates without ceasing on materials long since provided by scientific economy, and there seeks plausible explanations of the most obtrusive phenomena, for bourgeois daily use, but for the rest confines itself to systematising in a pedantic way, and proclaiming for everlasting truths, the trite ideas held by the self-complacent bourgeoisie with regard to their own world, to them the best of all possible worlds' (I: 81).

5. Here empiricism is quite useless as a means to scientific knowledge. Every individual views the world, including its economic phenomena, through social eyes, as an integral part of a definite network of social relations formed historically on the basis of human labour. And because this is so, 'Socio-historical properties of things very often merge in the eyes of the individual with their natural properties, while transitory properties of things and of man himself begin to seem eternal properties bound up with the very essence of things. These fetishistic naturalistic illusions (commodity fetishism is only one example) and the abstractions expressing them cannot therefore be refuted by mere indication of things given in contemplation' (Ilyenkov 1982: 127).

6. 'Political economists have laid it down as an axiom that Capital, the form of property at present predominant, is eternal; they have tasked their brains to show that capital is coeval with the world, and that it has no beginning, so it can have no end. In proof

of which astonishing assertion all the manuals of political economy repeat with much complacency the story of the savage who, having in his possession a couple of bows, lends one of them to a brother savage, for a share of the produce of the chase. So great were the zeal and ardour which economists brought to bear on their search for capitalist property in prehistoric times, that they succeeded, in the course of their investigations, in discovering the existence of property outside the human species, to wit amongst the invertebrates: for the ant, in her foresight, is a hoarder of provisions. It is a pity that they should not have gone a step farther, and affirmed that, if the ant lays up stores, she does so with a view to sell the same and realise a profit by the circulation of her capital' (Lafargue 1975).

7. Strictly speaking variable capital is equivalent to the total wage bill of productively-employed workers, that is workers producing surplus value, and not to that of all workers. So figures such as that for the share of wages in the national income cannot tell us anything directly about such things as the rate of exploitation. The distinction between productive and unproductive labour will be discussed in the next chapter; but there is an indication that the categories of Marx's *Capital* do not correspond immediately to empirical data.

8. Economists continually argue amongst themselves about the essential qualities of money. It is conventional to say that money has four functions: (a) as a means of exchange; (b) as a standard of value; (c) as a means of payment; and (d) as a store of value. It was Keynes who laid particular stress on this latter function, making it the basis for his theory of interest: interest was the payment for not hoarding. On the other hand, adherents to the quantity theory of money place their prime emphasis on money's role as a medium of exchange. Efforts to arrive at the essence of money by means of registering its functions are bound to fail in that they actually stand the real issue on its head. Its functions turn out to be not the manner in which the essential quality of money appears but, on the contrary, the condition from which its nature is deduced. The point is that money manifests several related but contradictory aspects within the capitalist system; to take one aspect, as expressed in one particular function, is bound to lead to an abstract and erroneous conception of money. Thus in the case of mercantilism, an absolute was made of money's function as a store of wealth and this paved the way for the identification of money with gold and silver. In recent years, at the time of mounting criticism of the position occupied by the dollar in the world monetary system, economists such as Jacques Rueff in France advocated the restoration of the Gold Standard, forgetting that this Standard operated under specific historical conditions during the last century which were incapable of resurrection in the present. On the other hand, those theories which hold that money is purely a convention, employed as a means of fixing relative prices, are equally one-sided. They lead to the conclusion that paper money, rather than the precious metals, are the ideal money-form. Paper money is, however, but one specific form of money and one which arises from its function as means of exchange. The point is that the various functions of money cannot merely be listed but must be considered in their real interconnection.

9. An early example of this was John Strachey (1938), who saw a close analogy between Marx's theory of the declining rate of profit and Keynes' notion of the declining marginal efficiency of capital.

10. The mystery of capital consists in the following: How can things (stocks of raw materials, bank balances, machinery and equipment, etc.) so different in appearance be united under the same head as 'capital'? And second, what is the secret of capital's ability to expand in value? For an historical account of the various, ultimately futile, efforts on the part of orthodox economics to answer these questions, see Shemyatenkov (1981).

11. At one point Joan Robinson rightly observes that 'Technical and physical relations, between man and nature, must be distinguished from social relations between man and man' (Robinson 1960: v). This is indeed the nub of the issue, but it is clear from what she says elsewhere that the real significance of the distinction has eluded her.

12. Joan Robinson suggests that Keynes had a quite new and revolutionary view of capital: 'The whole elaborate structure of the metaphysical justification for profit was blown up when he pointed out that capital yields a return not because it is productive but because it is scarce.' That income arises in connection with a good or service which is naturally

or artificially scarce is one of the central features of orthodox rent theory and in this respect Keynes was saying little new. Just as land yields a rent not because it is in scarce supply but because it is privately owned, so the return to various instruments of production reflects not their scarcity but their private ownership as capital. On the similarities between Joan Robinson's views on capital and those of Proudhon, see Rosdolsky (1977).

13. Given the time that he was engaged in his polemics with Malthus (the early years of the nineteenth century) Ricardo was to an extent justified in assuming that capitalism could develop the productive forces in a smooth crisis-free manner. Such an assumption became far less tenable as the century progressed.

14. The point is that while the world is given to man in sensation it cannot be comprehended through sensation. Empirical material is a necessary component of knowledge and in this sense Marxism is in no way hostile to the study of empirical material; indeed, such study is essential. Marx's *Capital*, for instance, involved the exhaustive study of a mass of factual material over a period of some 25 years. But the study of empirical material requires concepts and categories which have to be consciously developed. Those who imagine that they are dealing with 'the facts' and the facts alone, invariably operate with the most crass categories of thought which have been uncritically assimilated from bourgeois thought.

15. This involves a conception of the idea of contradiction. In general it can be said that positivism sees in contradiction an error in thought and views the development of thought as always involving the elimination of contradiction. Marxism, on the contrary, sees contradiction as the most vital property of the object itself, and the essential task of scientific thought to be not the elimination of contradiction through the redefinition of terms but as the uncovering of real contradictions and an analysis of their real solution. On this question, see Pilling (1980).

16. Joan Robinson appears not to take this extreme position for 'The concept of equilibrium, of course, is an indispensable tool of analysis' (1962: 81).

4 KEYNESIANISM, STATE SPENDING AND THE 'ARMS ECONOMY'

Ancient Egypt was doubly fortunate and doubtless owed to this its fabled wealth in that it possessed two activities, namely pyramid-building as well as the search for the precious metals, the fruits of which, since they could not serve the needs of man by being consumed, did not stale with abundance. (GT: 131)

One of the most obvious features associated with the nature of post-war capitalism has been the significant rise in public or state spending. Whatever measure one adopts, the increases have been dramatic — in the case of Britain from some 25 per cent of GNP in the pre-war period in over 50 per cent by the mid-1970s, according to one typical estimate. And the trend has been the same in all the major capitalist countries, though it has proceeded at differing speeds. Keynesianism made such spending respectable by arguing that it was one of the principal means available to protect the economy against undue fluctuations in activity. Indeed, the view that we now live in a 'mixed economy' with its public and private sectors became one of the main strands in social democratic thinking and one which was held to demonstrate the irrelevance of Marxism in modern conditions. Such is the strength of reaction against Keynesianism that it is now claimed that this spending has been both the source of the inflationary pressures which erupted in the early 1970s as well as of the slow growth in the British economy consequent on the diversion of spending from 'productive' to 'unproductive' spheres.

As far as Marxism is concerned, the issue of state spending has been the subject of much recent controversy. Some Marxists have argued that state spending has had a stabilising effect on post-war capitalist economy. They have claimed that such spending is either an essential precondition for capitalist equilibrium in so far as it provides various forms of socialisation, training, etc. (Gough *et al.*); or that it has the effect of counteracting the tendencies towards stagnation to which capital is allegedly prone (Baran and Sweezy; the various proponents of the permanent arms economy thesis). Others have argued that state spending, while necessary for capitalism, is none the less a drain on surplus value and that far from resolving the contradictions of capitalism it must, certainly in the long run, serve to aggravate those contradictions (Mattick, Yaffe, Fine and Harris).

Each of these positions involves a certain conception of the distinction between productive and unproductive expenditure. As is clear from the quotation from *The General Theory* which opened this chapter, Keynes also took a definite stand on this matter: he regarded all expenditure as being equally productive on the grounds that it would, via the process of the multiplier, raise the level of national income and employment. Here, as in most other respects, he followed the path of neoclassical economics, which holds that all labour, if it finds a reward in the market, is, by definition, productive. In other words, Keynes adopted the normal ahistorical view of bourgeois economics that quite fails to distinguish between what is productive 'in general' and what is productive for capital. That Keynes did accept this position is clear from the following passage:

> unemployment relief financed by loans is more readily accepted than the financing of improvements at a charge below the current rate of interest; whilst the form of digging holes in the ground known as gold-mining, which not only adds nothing whatever to the real wealth of the world but involves the disutility of labour, is the most acceptable of all solutions. If the Treasury were to fill old bottles with banknotes, bury them at suitable depths in disused coal-mines which are then filled up to the surface with town rubbish, and leave it to private enterprise on well-tried principles of *laissez-faire* to dig the notes up again (the right to do so being obtained, of course by tendering for leases of the note-bearing territory), there need be no more unemployment and with the help of the repercussions, the real income of the community, and its capital wealth also, would probably become a good deal greater than it actually is. It would indeed be more sensible to build houses and the like but if there are political and practical difficulties in the way of this, the above would be better than nothing. (GT: 129; cf. ibid.: 219–20)

The worker digging holes in the road and paid by the state is, from the point of view of his impact on the national income, of the same order as a worker employed in capitalist enterprise and producing surplus value. Such is Keynes' view of the matter.

Productive Labour in the History of Economics

In order to clarify the impact of state spending on capitalist economy, let us review briefly the ideas of economics about the nature of productive labour. For it was from a critical examination of their theoretical work that Marx's conception was developed.

In the period when the paramount need of the ascending bourgeoisie was to accumulate liquid capital, mercantilism was able, with some historical justification, to regard that labour which led to the accumulation of treasure as alone productive. Once industrial capital gains dominance over mercantile capital — once, that is, the production of surplus value rather than its mere redistribution through trade emerges as the principal economic activity — the notion of mercantilism to the effect that surplus value arises 'upon alienation' (through trade) is rejected. Attention now swings to the sphere of production, and in particular to an analysis of the capital–labour relationship.

The Physiocrats were the first to give any systematic treatment to the question of productive labour; the work of this school was decisive because although its basic area of concern was the agricultural sector of the economy — in France at that time predominantly feudal in kind — it none the less examined this sector from the standpoint of the emerging relations of capital. The Physiocrats came to the conclusion that agricultural labour was alone productive and they were further of the opinion that the future of the French economy hinged upon the activities of the farmer, for no other labour apart from that expended on the land played any role in the generation of the *'produit net'* (surplus value) out of which further accumulation alone could come. Despite the fact that in the Physiocratic conception lay the fetishised notion that the privileged position accorded to agricultural labour was taken as an expression of the productive power of the soil, it was of considerable historical significance precisely because it represented the first effort to investigate the processes of production rather than those of circulation. But because there was a confusion in the work of Physiocrats, namely one between natural phenomena (the power of the earth) and social phenomena (the specific historical form in which the natural world was confronted), the Physiocratic conception reduced itself to the elaboration of a correct state policy: How could a greater surplus be made available? Excessive state spending was amongst those misguided economic activities which for this school served to dissipate the surplus needed for capital accumulation.

Of all the political economists, Adam Smith paid greatest attention to the question of productive and unproductive labour. This was no accident. For Smith's theoretical work took place against the background of the manufacturing stage of the development of capitalism, in the period immediately prior to the appearance of large-scale industry. Industrial capital had yet to win its final victory over the landlord, moneylenders and others. Smith was more than anything concerned with the fate of the economic surplus (surplus value). He was worried lest it be wasted in the upkeep of state functionaries, not to say those many professions: jesters, opera singers, churchmen, the monarchy which, judged from the standpoint of capital, involved the expenditure of unproductive labour. All these groups were taken by Smith as being of the same order as domestic servants. The income they received involved a drain on surplus value. Marx summed up this point when he said that Smith spoke in

> the language of the still revolutionary bourgeoisie, which had not yet subjected to itself the whole of society, the state, etc. The state, Church, etc. are only justified in so far as they are committees to superintend or administer the common interests of the productive bourgeoisie and their costs — since by their nature these costs belong to the overhead cost of production — must be reduced to the unavoidable minimum. (Th: I)

Smith shared at least one concern with the Physiocrats, for like them he was aware of the harmful effects of unproductive consumption on the tempo of capital accumulation. As we have already seen, Smith's advance over the Physiocrats lay in the fact that he was interested not merely in the material foundations of production but specifically in the social forms which it assumed. Thus for Smith it was no longer a matter of selecting a particular type of concrete labour and elevating this to the rank of sole productive labour; he regarded all labour which exchanges against capital as being productive. Smith's step forward, one which has important implications for a consideration of Keynes, was that he drew a distinction between labour exchanging directly against capital (productive labour) and labour exchanging against the various forms of revenue (wages, profit, rent etc., i.e. unproductive labour). Only labour which by its consumption assists in the self-expansion of capital, is, from a capitalist standpoint, really productive. The second type of labour, that exchanging against revenue, constitutes a drain on surplus value and is therefore a source for the diminution of the rate of capital accumulation. Thus, to give an example from Smith, a tailor working in a capitalist enterprise and producing surplus value is a productive labourer. A tailor working in the household of a capitalist is quite unproductive. This is so because his income (his wage) is paid out of surplus value already created. In other words, in this case, the consumption of the capitalist impedes the production of surplus value, a truth reflected in the fact that capitalism — at least in its relatively early phases — is characterised by great frugality on the part of the owners of capital. (It is not suggested that Smith was unambiguous on this issue of productive and unproductive labour. In fact he eclectically combines this view of unproductive labour with the vulgar, commonsense, view that productive labour is that which is realised in a saleable commodity.)

Ricardo, writing in the period of a more fully developed capitalism, agreed with Smith's basic distinction between revenue (income) and capital as the indispensable criterion for distinguishing between productive and unproductive labour. But unlike Smith, Ricardo was concerned not so much with the absolute numbers of productive and unproductive workers as with the productivity of the former group. Ricardo drew a distinction between gross and net revenue:

> the whole produce of land and labour of every country is divided into three portions: of these one portion is devoted to wages, another to profits and the other to rent. It is from the last two portions only, that any deductions can be made for taxes or for savings, the former, in constituting all the necessary expenses of production provides [the nation's] net real income, its rent and profits, it is of no importance whether it consists of ten or twelve million inhabitants. Its power of supporting fleets and armies and all species of unproductive labour, must be in proportion to its net and not its gross revenue. (DR: 1)

Unlike many of those current commentators who have returned to the long-ignored theme of productive labour, Ricardo recognised that one of the key indices of capitalist development was the extent to which a declining number of productive workers could, because of improvements in technology, sustain a growing number of non-productive workers. (In this respect, those who 'blame' the capitalist crisis on the fact that too many workers are unproductively employed fall below the level of Ricardo and repeat some of the far less profound propositions of Adam Smith.) Thanks to the continual advance of productive techniques, the rate of profit could be maintained, said Ricardo, because such technical progress tended to depress the value of workers' subsistence and hence raise profits. We have seen that for Ricardo the fundamental reason for any capitalist breakdown lay not in the irreconcilable internal contradictions of the system, but solely because it runs up against the barrier of nature. But Ricardo somewhat modified this optimistic stance. For he moved towards the conclusion that the introduction of machinery might prove injurious to the interests of the workers, thereby marking the first decisive break in Adam Smith's generally harmonious view of the capitalist system.

Accumulation involves the economising of unproductive expenditures, but the introduction of machinery might well reduce the demand for labour. Here was a potential conflict between employment and accumulation, a fact first alluded to by Ricardo and one which has haunted economics to this day. Ricardo avoided the problems into which his scientific endeavours had led him by the simple device of postulating full employment, that is by means of an uncritical acceptance of Say's law. Having in his very premises ruled out of court the possibility of unemployment, Ricardo was able to concentrate on the other aspects of his conclusion — that the growth of unproductive expenditures was harmful to the accumulation of capital.

It was Malthus who sought to stress and bring into sharp relief the contradiction between the process of capital accumulation and that of employment, clearly a central theme for Keynes. Malthus argued that since workers were held to a subsistence level of wages and as capitalists tended to accumulate a large proportion of their income, the productive expenditures of the landlord as well as those of the state official, which had been the object of such scorn on Smith's part, were, in point of fact, essential if a glut of commodities was to be avoided. This notion of the necessity, and indeed the virtue, of unproductive consumption was bound up with the adding-up theory of value which Malthus derived from the 'weak', vulgar, side of Smith. Malthus held that if capitalist profit arises from 'overcharging' it is logically impossible for the worker to purchase the equivalent of the whole of his produce. Thus, according to Malthus, demand must always, in the nature of things, stand below supply. If a general overproduction of commodities was to be avoided it was required that the deficiency of demand be repaired by those standing outside the capital–labour relation. Adam Smith's unproductive workers were introduced as an artefact to resolve this problem. Malthus had established, so he believed, a sound theoretical base for an inflated state bureaucracy and a well-maintained Church.

Malthus posed the matter in the following manner. It is one which anticipates Keynes in many significant respects and helps to put the Keynesian 'revolution' into some historical perspective:

> under a rapid accumulation of capital, or, more properly speaking, a rapid conversion of unproductive into productive labour, the demand, compared with the supply of material products, would prematurely fail, and the motive for further accumulation checked, before it was checked by the exhaustion of the land. It follows that, without supposing the productive classes to consume much more than they are

found to do by experience, particularly when they are rapidly saving from their revenues to add to their capitals, it is absolutely necessary that a country with great powers of production should possess a body of unproductive consumers. (DR 2: 241)

And specifically on those sustained from taxes, Malthus made the following point:

Those which are supported by taxes are equally useful with regard to distribution and demand; they frequently occasion a division of property more favourable to the progress of wealth than would otherwise have taken place; they ensure that consumption which is necessary to give the proper stimulus to production; and the desire to pay a tax, and yet enjoy the same means of gratification, must often operate to excite the exertion of industry quite as effectually as the desire to pay a lawyer or physician. (ibid.: 432)

Moving now to Keynes. As we have already noted, not least amongst the consequences of the victory for the 'marginal revolution' during the last three decades of the nineteenth century was the loss of any critical distinction between productive and unproductive labour. The triumph of a theory of value — or what purported to be a theory of value — based on the principle of scarcity, meant a central emphasis was henceforth placed on the coordinate contribution of all the 'factors of production'. This necessarily precluded any separation of productive from unproductive labour. Indeed, the latter term could have no meaning. Any labour embodied in a good finding a purchaser on the market was by definition productive labour. Under capitalism there is no exploitation. Keynes, while repudiating Say's law of markets, accepted the neoclassical reformulation of value theory. He does, however, somewhat modify this position in making an implicit distinction between productive and unproductive consumption. Whereas in Smith and the classics generally productive consumption is that consumption of labour power which creates a surplus (surplus value), Keynes considered unproductive expenditure to be any in excess of the 'supply price' of a factor of production. Thus in the *Treatise* Keynes says:

We may define 'unproductive consumption' as consumption which could be forgone by the consumer without reacting on the amount of his productive effort, and 'productive consumption' as consumption which could not be forgone without such a reaction . . . so long as unemployment and unproductive consumption are allowed to exist side by side, present total net income and future total available income are less than they might be; and nothing is required to mend this situation except a method of transferring consumption from one set of individuals to another. (JMK CW: 6)

And further:

the evil of not creating wealth would be greater than the evil that wealth, when created, should not accrue to those who have made the sacrifice, namely, to the consumers whose consumption has been curtailed by the higher prices consequent on the Profit Inflation. (ibid.)

Keynes proceeded to explain that the mechanism for such a transfer was through a fall in real wages, that is, by means of a profit inflation. According to Keynes, workers bargain for a money wage rather than a real wage, from which fact he concluded that a rise in prices not accompanied by an increase in money wages does not reduce the supply of labour. On this basis the market price of labour power lies above its supply price and this excess of market over supply price constitutes unproductive consumption. The corollary of this position is that if each productive factor is paid at its supply price then the category of unproductive consumption disappears. (It was only on the basis of the separation of labour from the means of production that the supply price of the resultant commodity, labour power, could be determined. Keynes here takes as given the fact that labour power has a supply price, that is to say, he assumes what any serious analysis of capitalist economy is bound to explain.)

It should be clear from this brief survey that the Keynesian conception of unproductive consumption has little if anything in common with that of the classical economists and even less with that of Marx. Certainly as far as Marx was concerned, the fundamental question was not whether the price of labour power lies above or below its supply price but first why labour power should exist as a commodity and why the ability to perform labour should under certain historical-social conditions be transformed into a commodity, attach itself to a thing and thereby acquire a price. The nature, significance and origin of these facts either entirely eludes or, even worse, is completely unexamined in orthodox economics. The problem for Keynes concerned the particular prices at which these and other transactions took place. To have examined critically the conditions under which labour power becomes a commodity would have taken him in the direction of a thorough-going appraisal of bourgeois economics which was quite beyond his scope and aim.

State Expenditure: The Marxist Approach

As we know, the view prevalent in the last century, that all public expenditure was of an unproductive nature, with the rise of Keynesianism gave way to the proposition that public spending was just as beneficial as private capital investment, even where this was financed out of increased state indebtedness: both have the same positive impact on production and income. And if this should involve higher levels of state borrowing this did not matter, for the money could be recouped out of the higher income that the initial injection of state expenditure would produce in the next round. Writing in the mid-1960s, and analysing the post-war expansion of the American economy, Alvin Hansen, a leading Keynesian, could say:

> The events of the last fifteen years . . . reaffirm the long-standing lesson of history that growth requires an increase in money, credit and debt. And in the public–private economy of today, a well-balanced growth suggests an increase of debt at all levels — business debt, consumer debt, state and local debt, and federal debt. (Hansen 1964: 655–6)

On the face of it, such a conception seemed justified in the light of the post-war boom. State intervention in the economy, involving amongst other things increasing quantities of private and public debt, did coincide with a general expansion of capitalism. But this is just the point: this was only the outward, superficial appearance of the matter. For it by no means follows that the first phenomenon (increased state involvement in the economy and growing debt) was the cause of the second (the longish period of relatively crisis-free extended reproduction after 1945). Nor is the reverse the case, namely that a decrease in public spending can necessarily provide the basis for a renewed period of expansion within capitalism, as the advocates of 'sound finance' claim to be the case. No amount of empirical work can of itself yield an answer to this question: the real impact of state spending on the functioning of capitalism must first of all be evaluated from the theoretical angle. And this in turn involves a definite conception as to the nature of capitalist economy.[1]

We can start from the basic proposition that state spending is financed in one of two ways. It is paid for either out of taxes or is financed by loans made by the state. In practice the cost of such spending is usually met by a combination of these means. Let us therefore analyse the role of taxation from the point of view of the Marxist notion of unproductive expenditure. Marx's analysis of capitalism rests upon the proposition that net wages constitute the price of labour power. Naturally, because labour power is a commodity its price can and does fluctuate in response to the changes in demand and supply conditions. But such fluctuations take place around a definite point. Wages are the price of labour power, the value of which is determined by the value of the necessary means of subsistence required to maintain the worker and his family, taking into account the historical conditions under which the labour power concerned is bought, sold and employed. Nor does Marx ignore the fact that the working class, through trade union and other forms of action, can raise the price of labour power, although he points out that there are definite limits to such action, the principal one being that such increases cannot move beyond the point where they endanger the process of capital accumulation. (Here is expressed the fact that Marx's theory of wages is by no means identical with the 'iron law of wages' generally subscribed to by the classical economists and which depended upon the Malthusian theory of population.[2])

Unless this proposition is accepted — unless, that is to say, we commence from the basic assumption that net money wages do represent the price of labour power — then it becomes impossible to explain the existence of surplus value in any theoretical sense. Surplus value would depend upon the ability of the capitalists to 'rob' the working class. This was the old 'force' theory held by many socialists prior to Marx. Just as in his theoretical investigation of capitalism Marx started from the assumption that all commodities were bought and sold at value, so he proceeded from the premise that labour power was similarly bought and sold at its value. The task was to reconcile the existence of surplus value with this law, not explain it in terms of its abrogation, as the Ricardian socialists and others had tended to do.

Now if we accept these propositions, then it follows automatically that all taxes are in the last resort deductions from surplus value. And this is true whether the taxes are levied on profits and dividends (where this is self-evidently the case) or on wages. In the latter case although the worker 'pays' the taxes — either as income tax or a tax on expenditure — they are none the less deductions from surplus value. This fundamental point has direct implications for our theoretical approach to the question of state spending. All state spending represents a deduction from surplus value: this is the basic Marxist proposition. As such it constitutes unproductive expenditure, in that only expenditure which sets in motion labour which in turn creates surplus value is productive from the point of view of capital. And this is so whether state spending is financed out of immediate taxation or out of loans. The latter instance is no different in principle, for whereas in the case where state spending is matched by an equivalent volume of surplus value in the form of taxes, in the latter case the state is obliged to make interest payments to the *rentier* to cover its borrowing.

We noted earlier that according to Mathews and others, Keynesian-type policies could not claim credit for the post-war boom, at least not in Britain, in that budget deficits were not run and, if anything, budgetary policy was deflationary in its impact on the economy. While this might lead us to the conclusion that Keynesianism was not practised in the post-war period, it by no means follows that the level of state spending was of no economic consequence. Quite the contrary is the case. The state cannot compete with private capital and therefore its main activity is confined to the provision of goods and services for 'public consumption'. And because such consumption is financed out of surplus value it must, other things being equal, involve a reduction in the rate of capital accumulation: for what is consumed by individuals cannot, in the nature of things, be accumulated. If such public consumption (road building, hospitals, schools, etc.) is financed out of state loans, this does not alter the matter in any fundamental way for now the burden is simply pushed into the future. In this case public consumption is financed out of future surplus value, or more strictly out of hoped-for surplus value.

In other words the 'mixed economy' is in reality an economy which produces surplus value (the private sector) but which at the same time supports a public sector financed out of state taxation. And resources devoted to the latter must in the final analysis be made at the expense of the former. Of course, from the point of view of his own profits, an individual capitalist does not mind whether he 'works' for the state or whether he sells his commodities on the market in the normal way. Indeed he may prefer the former in so far as his orders may be guaranteed for a long period and he may be able to sell his output at prices which yield him above-average profits. The analysis of capitalism cannot however proceed from the standpoint of the needs and interests of the individual capitalist but from the point of view of the system as a whole. If this latter viewpoint is adopted it is clear that while the individual firm producing goods for public consumption extracts surplus value from his labour force, this surplus value is not realised by exchange on the market against other commodities but is realised with money which the government has raised by means of taxation; in short, it is realised against surplus value which has already been created in another part of the economy. To presume that such state spending can be the means to the creation of surplus value is to indulge in double-counting.

Now it is of course true that if the state purchases goods which otherwise would go unproduced this will have the effect of raising employment, income and wealth. This is indeed the basis of Keynesian theory. This has to be considered from the point of view of certain of the most decisive trends in capitalist economy within the epoch of imperialism. The twentieth century is characterised by an intense concentration of production and capital leading to the predominance of monopoly, the merging of banking and industrial capital to form the foundation for finance capital. The accumulation of capital on this basis led capitalism to become 'overripe', to use Lenin's phrase, and resulted in the metropolitan countries in particular producing a 'surplus' of capital which was unable to find profitable investment outlets in the country concerned. This surplus capital is a very real phenomenon: it exists as chronic undercapacity production, in the accumulation of huge monetary reserves in both individual capitalist enterprises as well as in the banks, in the ever increasing scope for speculation on money and commodity markets, etc. and not least in the ever present striving for the export of capital. In this respect, profits on taxes represent the accumulation of this surplus capital in the state budget. And if the government drains off, by means of taxes on surplus value, a certain proportion of this surplus capital — the part which has not found profitable outlets elsewhere — it makes a demand on the product of private industry that leads to an expansion of total purchasing power and along with it incomes and employment. Hence it would be stupid not to allow for the fact that state action can, within certain limits, expand the scope of the domestic market beyond that which would obtain on the basis of the spontaneous circulation of capital. But it would be even more erroneous to see the state's power as without limit in this sphere. For this only serves to take us back to the most fundamental of all questions and one dealt with from various angles in the last chapter. The fact is that the level of income in capitalist society is, objectively, limited by the accumulation of capital. And only if the general conditions for the accumulation of capital are sound can the state, even to a limited extent, raise the level of national income by means of fiscal policies.

The real question at issue here is this: Is the capitalist system one founded on the production of goods and services to satisfy human needs, or is it one based on the production of surplus value in which the production of use values is purely incidental to the process? As we know Marx answers this latter question in the affirmative. The production of wealth takes place only in so far as the production of surplus value takes place. So to the extent that goods, wealth and income are, via public spending, generated at the expense of surplus value, far from alleviating the crisis of capitalism such spending must only serve to aggravate its underlying contradiction — which takes the form of an inability to generate sufficient profit on the capital currently in existence. In financing its activities the state creams off a portion of surplus value from private capital. Even if we assume that taxation were reduced and private investment increased by an equivalent amount this would not necessarily lead to an increase in surplus value. For this would depend entirely on the conditions of production, the conditions for the extraction of surplus value, etc. Only by a concrete examination of these conditions can that question be answered one way or the other. If, on the other hand, the surplus value which was otherwise creamed off by the state was to lie idle in the hands of the capitalists this could clearly lead to no increase in surplus value. For such surplus value would no longer be capital but merely a hoard.

So far it has been assumed that state spending has been financed out of taxation. In practice this is not the case. Although for a period after the last war the state did cover much of its spending from tax revenues, from the mid-1970s onwards it has been forced to borrow on an increasing scale. The fact that state spending is covered out of budget deficits does not alter the substance of the argument presented above; it merely complicates the appearance of the situation somewhat. Should the state run a budget deficit this has to be financed in some way: the state has to balance its books by borrowing. But this borrowing, like taxes, is a drain on surplus value. The money capital utilised by the government is not invested as capital but disappears from the system in the form of public consumption. As Marx says, 'Interest-bearing capital remains as such only so long as the loaned capital is actually converted into capital and a surplus is produced with it, of which interest is a part' (III: 374). From this point of view the interest-bearing 'capital' involved in the financing of the state debt in the shape of interest payments to bond-holders is not real capital but what Marx calls fictitious or illusory capital. For it is not invested in productive activities which yield surplus value. Marx poses the issue in the following manner when speaking of illusory capital:

The sum that was lent to the state no longer has any kind of existence. It was never designed to be spent as capital to be invested, and yet only by being invested as capital could it have made itself into self-maintaining value. . . . No matter how these transactions are multiplied, the capital of the national debt remains purely fictitious, and the moment these promissory notes become unsaleable, the illusion of this capital disappears. (III: 595–6)

Again, if we adopt the standpoint of the individual capitalist the matter appears to be quite the opposite and straightforward. As an individual, the capitalist cares not one iota whether on the one hand his income is derived from capital invested in industry and is thus the means for the generation of surplus value or whether, on the other, it arises from money loaned to the government and bringing him a return, which, given the laws of competition, and taking into account the degree of risk involved, must tend towards the average rate of profit on capital as a whole. (Indeed, other things being equal, the owner of capital might prefer to take his surplus value in the form of interest paid by the government on the grounds that this appears safer, based as it is on the strength of the state and given that holding state bonds does not involve the risk of committing one's capital to industrial production.) But if we commence, not from the consciousness of the individual capitalist, but from the objective laws (the 'being') of the economy as a whole, capitalism cannot be indifferent about this matter. This is so because the ultimate basis of the capitalist economy remains industrial production. The stability of capital rests upon its ability to extract surplus value in the course of industrial production.

Industrial capital is the only mode of existence of capital in which not only the appropriation of surplus-value, or surplus product, but simultaneously its creation is a function of capital. Therefore with it the capitalist mode of production is a necessity. Its existence implies the class antagonism between capitalists and wage-labourers. To the extent that it seizes control of social production, the technique and social organisation of the labour-process are revolutionised and with them the economico-historical type of society. The other types of capital which appeared before industrial capital amid conditions of social production that have receded into the past or are now succumbing, are not subordinated to it and the mechanism of their functions altered in conformity with it, but move solely with it as their basis, hence live and die, stand and fall with this basis. Money-capital and commodity capital, so far as they function as vehicles of particular branches of business, side by side with industrial capital, are nothing but modes of existence of different functional forms now assumed, now discarded, by industrial capital in the sphere of circulation — modes which, due to social division of labour, have attained independent existence and been developed one-sidedly. (II: 55)

And again:

> Money-capital, commodity-capital, and productive capital do not therefore designate independent kinds of capital whose functions form the content of likewise independent branches of industry separated from one another. They denote here only special functional forms of industrial capital, which assumes all three of them one after another. (II: 53)

It is quite true to say that so long as capital is accumulating at an appropriate rate the system as a whole can stand the existence of a certain portion of surplus value drainage in the form of interest paid on state bonds. For much of the post-war boom, although the public debt of the major capitalist countries was increasing, it was growing at a rate less than the accumulation of capital. Although this in no way altered the nature of such state debts the situation was containable. It is only when the specific weight of such debt begins to mount, when it threatens to consume a greater proportion of a shrinking or only slowly rising volume of surplus value, that the situation becomes intolerable for capitalism. Then the needs of the individual capitalist with his share in the state debt and the need of the system as a whole to extract surplus value in the course of industrial production come into conflict. Marx sums up the point at issue in the following passage; it makes clear that there are definite limits to the ability of capital to assume the form of money capital. Marx points out that while the individual owner of capital does not concern himself about the form of his surplus value,

> This is correct in the practical sense for the individual capitalist. He has the choice of making use of his capital by lending it out as interest-bearing capital, or expanding its value on his own by using it as productive capital. . . . But to apply it to the total capital of society, as some vulgar economists do, and to go so far as to define it as the cause of profit, is, of course, preposterous. The idea of converting all the capital into money-capital without there being people who buy and put to use means of production, which make up the total capital outside a relatively small portion existing in money [i.e. gold] is, of course, sheer nonsense. It would be still more absurd to presume that capital would yield interest on the basis of capitalist production without performing any productive function, i.e. without creating surplus-value, of which interest is just a part; that the capitalist mode of production would run its course without capitalist production. (III: 370)

Here lies the key to understanding the fallacy of the Keynesian view that the size of the public debt was of little or no consequence, given the fact that it was debt 'we owed ourselves'.

Arms Expenditure[3]

Spending on armaments is regarded by some writers as constituting the major source of the post-war capitalist boom.[4] Because for a time this theory exercised a certain degree of influence in radical circles and because it was essentially a variant upon Keynesianism (though often decked out in what purported to be Marxist terminology) we shall say something specifically about it. Harman (1983) provides a resumé of the essential points of this theory, which often goes under the label of the 'permanent arms economy'. The fact that he is an advocate of this theory makes his rehearsal of its main points doubly useful. He summarises the version of the theory proposed by Michael Kidron in the following manner:

> Kidron points out that there has always been one way in which capitalists use surplus value which prevents it being used to expand the means of production: when they invest in luxury goods for their own consumption. He suggests that spending by the state on arms — which has expanded enormously this century — should be regarded in the same way. (Harman 1984: 39)

Further, according to Harman (here again following Kidron), Marx, writing in the conditions of the nineteenth century, did not analyse the role of luxury production. In fact Marx assumed

> a closed system in which all output flows back as inputs in the form of investment goods or wage goods. There are no leaks. Yet in principle a leak could insulate the compulsion to grow from its most important consequences. . . . In such a case there would be no decline in the average rate of profit, no reason to expect increasingly severe slumps and so on. (ibid.)

An immediate response to Harman is that it is a strange sort of capitalism which produces only wage goods and investment goods! Where does the consumption of the owners of capital enter the picture? Capitalism does after all involve precisely what Harman charges Marx with having ignored, namely the consumption on the part of those who take no part in the process of production. As we shall see, the charge that Marx ignored the consumption of the capitalist is in any event quite false. But this apart, according to Harman and Kidron, luxury goods production, is, from the theoretical angle, to be treated as equivalent to arms production. In order to examine the basis of the theory of the arms economy and establish that it is indeed of a fundamentally Keynesian character, we can follow Kidron and Harman on this point. As we have established, the key feature of Marx's distinction between productive and unproductive labour was this: that it had nothing at all to do with the resulting commodity, that is with the use value of the product which entered the market. Here Marx clashed with the vulgar economist who insisted that everything, precisely because it had a use value, must, by definition, be the result of productive labour. Now whether the labour expended on the production of luxuries (that is on articles produced for the consumption of the bourgeoisie) is productive, for Marx rests upon one and only one consideration: Did its consumption result in the direct production of surplus value? In this respect the fact that the good is a luxury has nothing whatsoever to do with the essence of the matter. From the point of view of capital, the production of luxury liners can be equally productive of surplus value as can the production of bread. So the production of luxuries cannot be separated from the production and circulation of commodities as a whole within capitalist economy, nor can such production be considered apart from the basis on which the economy as a whole rests: the production of surplus value.

Now why, according to Harman, should goods produced in the so-called Department III (luxury goods production) be distinguished from other goods?

> Such goods, by definition, do not enter into 'productive consumption'. Goods which form part of the means of production pass on their value to new goods as they are consumed in the production process. Goods which form part of the real wage of workers pass on their value as workers who consume them create value and surplus value. Goods which are consumed in one way or another by the capitalists end their life without passing their value on to anything else. (Harman 1984: 40)

Just as Keynes' pyramids do not 'stale with age', so luxury goods do not have any impact on the formation of the average rate of profit and its movement, except in the negative sense that they serve to arrest the fall in the rate of profit. But what Harman says here is sheer nonsense from the standpoint of Marx's most fundamental conception of capitalist economy. Of course the labour socially necessary for the production of constant capital (machinery, raw materials, etc.) is passed on in the course of production. The value embodied in such constant capital is absorbed into the commodities which are realised in the course of the production process. But this can take place only because of the active element in that process — labour power. All commodities, this one apart, play a purely passive role in the process of production. The fact that workers consume articles of subsistence is of course necessary for the production of surplus value in that should the workers starve there would naturally be no surplus value. This is hardly a profound conclusion. But the consumption of such means of subsistence, indispensable though it is, is not the source of surplus value, as Harman appears to suggest. The real question is this: if the labour employed in the production process creates commodities (such commodities can assume the form of any material objects, or none at all) which embody surplus value, then such surplus value cannot but participate in the formation of the average rate of profit. For this rate is determined by the total capital (c + v) compared with the total surplus value (s) throughout the economy as a whole. To argue otherwise is to abandon Marx's basic contention that capital is motivated by one thing only: the creation of surplus value. For capitalism, the production of use values (material production) is a necessary nuisance, one which 'ideally' it would like to get rid of, reducing the process of capital accumulation to the circuit M−M′, that is, one in which the intervening stage of production is eliminated. (Needless to say, this it can never achieve.)

Now did Marx ignore unproductive consumption, as Kidron suggests? Quite the opposite is the case. For far from ignoring such consumption Marx analysed its necessity and why it tended to grow with the development of the productive forces. In order to establish this fact and to make clear Marx's approach to the questions discussed in this part of the argument we can refer to a passage from his 'Results of the Immediate Process of Production' where the following is found:

> A large part of the annual product which is consumed as revenue and hence does not re-enter production as its means consists of the most tawdry products (use-values) designed to gratify the most impoverished appetites and fancies. As far as the question of productive labour is concerned, however, the nature of these objects is quite irrelevant (although obviously the development of wealth would inevitably receive a check if a disproportionate part were to be reproduced in this way

instead of being changed back into the means of production and subsistence, to become absorbed once more — productively consumed, in short — into the process of reproduction either of commodities or of labour-power). This sort of productive labour produces use-values and objectifies itself in products that are destined only for unproductive consumption. In their reality they have no use-value for the process of reproduction. . . ordinary economic theory finds it impossible to utter a sensible word on the barriers to the production of luxuries even from the standpoint of capitalism itself. The matter is very simple, however, if the elements of the process of reproduction are examined systematically. If the process of reproduction suffers a check, or if its progress, in so far as this is already determined by the natural growth of the population, is held up by the disproportionate diversion of productive labour into unproductive articles, it follows that the means of subsistence or production will not be reproduced in the necessary quantities. In that event it is possible to condemn the production of luxury goods from the standpoint of capitalist production. For the rest, however, luxury goods are absolutely necessary for a mode of production which creates wealth for the non-producer and which therefore must provide that wealth in forms which permit its acquisition only by those who enjoy. (Marx 1976: 1045–6)

At one point (despite denials of the fact at other stages in his argument), Harman is obliged to admit that Marx did recognise the growth of unproductive consumption, with which the development of capitalism was associated. Thus he quotes Marx:

As capitalist production grows, accumulation and wealth become developed, the capitalist ceases to be the mere incarnation of capital. The progress of capitalist production not only creates a world of delights; it lays open in speculation and the credit system, a thousand sources of individual enrichment. When a certain stage of development has been reached, a conventional degree of prodigality, which is also an exhibition of wealth and consequently a source of credit, becomes necessary. . . . Luxury enters into the expenses of representation. (I: 544)

In commenting on this passage Harman says:

Thus Marx suggests in passing in *Capital* that capitalism, which initially flourished through the destruction of preceding societies with their vast superstructure of unproductive classes, becomes sluggish as it becomes old and thereby creates its own non-productive superstructure. (ibid.: 43)

Here Harman's procedure is quite unhistorical. First, in the passage he quotes from Marx the point is that in the last century, in the period when capitalism was still able to develop the productive forces in a manner which was relatively crisis-free, the growth of what Harman calls a non-productive superstructure was an expression of this development and in no sense an 'escape route' for capital. The fact that capital could sustain a growing layer of middle-class personnel who were not directly engaged in productive activities was an expression of its vigour. But when the twentieth century is reached, the epoch of imperialism, the situation is quite different. Lenin criticised Hilferding for many weaknesses in his work: one of them was his failure to examine the parasitic nature of capitalism as a whole in the present epoch. (Here Hilferding the 'Marxist' fell below the level of Hobson the radical liberal who had dealt with this issue, in connection with the Boer War for instance.) This is how Lenin posed the issue:

As we have seen. the deepest economic foundation of imperialism is monopoly. This is capitalist monopoly, i.e., monopoly which has grown out of capitalism and which exists in the general environment of capitalism, commodity production and competition, in permanent and insoluble contradiction to this general environment. Nevertheless, like all monopoly, it inevitably engenders a tendency towards stagnation and decay. Since monopoly prices are established, even temporarily, the motive cause of technical, and consequently, of all other progress disappears to a certain extent and, further, the economic possibility arises of deliberately retarding technical progress. (Lenin 1969: 241)

And Lenin went on to point to the connection between the (relative) tendency towards stagnation on the one hand and the growth of an increasing proportion of the capitalist class whose capital was not engaged in the productive process.

Further, imperialism is an immense accumulation of money capital in a few countries . . . hence the extraordinary growth of a class, or rather a stratum of *rentiers*, i.e. people who live by 'clipping coupons', who take no part in any enterprise whatever, whose profession is idleness. The export of capital, one of the most essential economic bases of imperialism, still more completely isolates the *rentiers* from production and sets the seal of parasitism on the whole country that lives by exploiting the labour of several overseas countries and colonies. (ibid.)

Quoting figures from Hobson dealing with the income from trade as against that yielded by foreign investments, Lenin comments, 'The income of the *rentiers* is five times greater than the income obtained from the foreign trade of the biggest "trading" country in the world! This is the essence of imperialism and imperialist parasitism' (ibid.). And drawing attention to the increasingly widespread use of the term *'rentier* state' in analyses of imperialism: 'The *rentier* state is a state of parasitic, decaying capitalism, and this circumstance cannot fail to influence all the socio-political conditions of the countries concerned, in general, and the two fundamental trends in the working-class movement, in particular' (ibid.: 243).

So the growth of 'unproductive expenditures' did not constitute an 'escape route' for capitalism along the lines envisaged by Harman. In these passages and in his study of imperialism as a whole, Lenin is drawing attention to the fact that this parasitism cannot be divorced from the overall crisis of capitalism in this epoch. The export of money capital and the export of capital generally, as far as Lenin was concerned, was one of the most potent sources of war in the twentieth century as capital was driven to divide and redivide the world market and the total available stock of capital among the various monopoly interests.

(Here, incidentally, is revealed the thoroughly shallow nature of Keynes' 'attack' on the *rentier* capitalist. Keynes wanted to remove such elements while leaving the system as whole intact. Naturally he quite failed to see the connection between the rapid emergence of 'coupon clipping' and the overall decay and decline of capitalist economy. Like all petty bourgeois critics he wanted to remove certain unseemly features of capital while preserving its foundation. This is yet another expression of the eclecticism which lay behind his thinking as a whole.)

Another example Harman cites to justify the same essential theoretical position is that concerned with the growth of commercial activities. He reproduces a passage from Marx:

It is clear that as the scale of production is expanded, commercial operations required constantly for the recirculation of industrial capital multiply accordingly . . . the more developed the scale of production, the greater . . . the commercial operations of industrial capital. (III: 293)

According to Harman, this passage indicates that Marx saw 'with the expansion of the system industrial capital has to surrender an increasing amount of surplus value to finance the unproductive buying and selling of its output' (ibid.: 43). But again the point at issue is misconstrued. The growing division of labour amongst the various branches of capital in the last century was, at that specific period, an expression of the growth of the productive forces, an indication of the fact that just as the means of finance were increasingly beyond the range of even the largest capitalist so were the means of distribution. The greater share of capital going to those engaged (unproductively) in the realisation of surplus value testifies to the growth of the productive forces, indicates that they are pressing ever more against the limits of the private ownership of the means of production, signifies the fact, not of some ability on the part of capital to chart a course out of its historical dilemma, but establishes its impending historical demise. And the objective conditions for that demise are joined in the twentieth century when each capitalist power engages in ever greater parasitic activities, the main expression of this being the ever greater resources devoted to war and war preparations. In both these cases, that of unproductive consumption, especially state spending, and the expansion of commercial activities, Harman in fact stands reality diametrically on its head. In short he confuses effect with cause. Capital is able to expand expenditure under both these heads only to the extent that economic conditions allow (which concretely means the ability to extract surplus value at the required rate, or, especially in the present century, to seize the surplus value belonging to one's rivals). Once such conditions no longer hold — as in periods of mounting crisis — intense efforts are necessarily made to reduce such 'waste' while at the same time pressure for war is likewise intensified.

Investment and Consumption

The theory that arms expenditure represents one crucial way in which capitalism can overcome its contradictions depends, in the final analysis, on the view that the surplus capital which the system generates can be absorbed by means of state spending. As Harman puts it:

> The experiences of the First World War and the period 1933–45 was that, provided the competing groups of capitalists within any country allowed it, the capitalist state could intervene to ensure that production proceeded on an upward course — even if the rate of profit

declined. For the state could collect into its hands the mass of surplus value and direct it into investments, regardless of profitability. (Harman 1984: 78)

This thesis is essentially a variant on Keynesianism in that it holds that the tempo of capitalist development is ultimately dependent on the rate of capital investment. Keynesianism sees in periods of prosperity a tendency for overinvestment and in periods of slump a tendency towards underinvestment. (It was, of course, this latter question which exercised Keynes' attention.) By ironing out these fluctuations, by means of credit controls or direct state investment, capitalist economy can be stabilised. According to those who see in arms spending a means of capitalist stability, it is the ability of the system to invest in arms which allows it to escape from its old pattern of booms and slumps. This is the case because capital invested in arms, it is argued, does not take part in the formation of the average rate of profit. Many aspects of this thesis could be taken up, but one issue which it involves is that of the relationship of investment and consumption.

Now for Marxism the theory of reproduction is certainly based on the fundamental fact that the production of means of production (Department I industries) plays the leading role in capitalist development. Production grows principally on the basis of the growth of the means of the production, rather than the means of consumption, that is to say, on the more rapid rate of increase in Department I as against Department II. This is but another way of saying that the organic composition of capital (the ratio of constant to variable capital) tends to rise over time. The growth of personal consumption under capitalism follows the growth of productive consumption. But it fulfils one role in the production sphere, and another as the cause of the capitalist economic cycle. While the production of the means of production is certainly the most important moment in the investigation of the cyclical movement of capital, it is not the initial link, not the 'prime mover': the cause of capitalist crises is to be located in the laws and the contradictions of capitalist production, rather than in the specific features of the production and reproduction of the means of production.

It has long been held by certain economists that capital investment is a self-contained entity, quite independent of consumption in the capitalist process of reproduction. It is of course true that during the phases of recovery and especially in periods of prosperity the production of machinery, equipment, the build-up of stocks, etc. increases, while in the downturn the production of such items falls sharply, often more so than in the case of consumer goods. But it would be false to conclude from this undoubted empirical fact that the real source of capitalist crises is to be discovered in the movement of the level of capital investment, with its corollary that if some means could be discovered for damping down the fluctuations in the rate of investment the key to the regulation of capitalist economy as a whole would be to hand.

It was the Russian legal Marxist, Tugan Baranovsky, proceeding, so he believed, from the Marxist reproduction schema, who argued that capitalist reproduction on an expanded scale was possible even where personal consumption fell absolutely or even ceased completely. That the development of capitalism could take place quite independently of the level of personal consumption was possible, Tugan Baranovsky held, because personal consumption could be replaced by the production of means of production alone. Starting from the correct point that there is a tendency for Department I to grow more rapidly than Department II, he took a false step in declaring the complete separation of production from consumption. In so far as Keynesianism gives currency to the idea that capital investment is a factor independent of the level of consumption, a self-contained factor in the process of reproduction, it follows the same path as Tugan Baranovsky, although not necessarily drawing its conclusions as sharply.

The significant thing to note here is that Harman shares this same position for he writes,

> One of the greatest followers of Marx, Rosa Luxemburg, could not understand how capitalism could continually expand without producing more goods for consumption. Similarly these Marxists [opponents of the theory of the permanent arms economy] could not understand how capitalism could possibly benefit from continually expanding the means of destruction. Like Rosa Luxemburg, they were so bemused by the irrationality of what capitalists were doing as to try to deny that this was how the system worked. (Harman 1984: 83)

According to Marx, the reproduction of fixed capital is the most important aspect explaining the length of the capitalist production cycle — 'fixed' not in the sense that capital is fixed in the instruments of labour but rather in the sense that a portion of the value laid out in instruments of labour remains fixed in them, while the other portion circulates as a component of the value of the product (see II: 202). The average length of time during which machinery and equipment are renewed constitutes the most important aspect explaining those long-term cycles through which industrial development has taken place since the creation of large-scale industry. The general reduction of commodity prices and a depression of the rate of profit in times of crisis increases enormously the pressure on entrepreneurs to reduce production costs. This is attempted by means of wage reductions. But this is by no means the only way. Capital in such periods strives to introduce more modern and efficient methods of production. Price reductions on equipment greatly depreciate ('de-valorise') existing capital, that is brings about what Marx calls its 'moral' depreciation before its physical deterioration has necessarily taken place. Weaker capitals, those less well placed to stand such pressures, will be eliminated, with the consequent further concentration and centralisation of capital. But such a crisis prepares the way for a renewal of fixed capital, providing the basis for a period of industrial prosperity when the replacement of fixed capital in turn lays the foundation for the growth of other branches of production. But one cannot conclude from this (simplified) review of Marx's theory that the reproduction of fixed capital or 'investment' constitutes a self-contained factor which, in itself, determines the nature of capitalist cycles and crises. On the contrary, for as Marx explains:

> Competition compels the replacement of the old instruments of labour by new ones before the expiration of their natural life, especially when decisive changes occur. Such premature renewals of factory equipment on a rather large social scale are mainly enforced by catastrophe and crises. (II: 170)

And further, 'But a crisis always forms the starting-point of large new investments. Therefore from the point of view of society as a whole, more or less, a new material basis for the next turnover cycle' (II: 186). Here Marx poses the matter in a manner which is diametrically opposed to that of Keynesianism, which sees in investment as such the key to the dynamic of the capitalist economy. For Marx it is the periodic crises of overproduction engendered by the inherent contradictions of capitalism which give rise to fluctuations in the rate of capital investment, and not the other way round. Crises are the means by which initial disproportions (in this case a disproportion between investment and consumption) are corrected, often in the most violent manner. So a collapse of investment which is characteristic of a slump is not the cause of such a slump but merely one of its consequences. Here is one more instance of the bankruptcy of positivism. The issue cannot be settled by discovering the degree of correlation between the phenomena concerned (here investment and the industrial cycle). Such a method can never provide the basis for a real explanation of the processes which have brought these appearances into being. This task requires theoretical analysis, a point which eludes Harman.

It was Lenin who developed Marx's work on the relationship of consumption to production within the capitalist system. In the first place it is a consequence of Marx's theory of realisation that the growth of means of production develops faster than the growth of consumer goods: 'Capitalist production, and, consequently, the home market, grow not so much on account of articles of consumption as on account of means of production. In other words, the increase in means of production outstrips the increase in articles of consumption' (LCW 3: 54). Production not only grows more rapidly than consumption but precedes it. Thus Lenin:

> To expand production (to 'accumulate' in the categorical meaning of the term) it is first of all necessary to produce means of production, and for this it is consequently necessary to expand that department of social production which manufactures means of production, it is necessary to draw into it workers who immediately present a demand for articles of consumption, too. Hence 'consumption' develops after 'accumulation', or after 'production'; strange though it may seem, it cannot be otherwise in capitalist society. (LCW 2: 155)

Now within certain limits, production is independent of consumption in that in the industries producing means of production an exchange takes place between firms within that department so that production, to a certain degree, creates its own market. But this independence is far from being absolute; on the contrary it is strictly relative and there is no basis for the contention that production can proceed indefinitely independently of consumption. From the fact that production of means of production tends to expand more rapidly than means of consumption

> in no way does it follow that the turning out of the means of production can develop completely independently of the production of articles of consumption and without any connection to it. . . . In the final analysis, therefore, productive consumption (the consumption of means of production) is always bound up with individual consumption and is always dependent on it. (LCW 4: 59)

Here is the key to rejecting Harman's thesis that capitalist production can develop independently of capitalist consumption, and its corollary that arms spending was the key to the longevity of the post-war boom.

What has been said in this chapter should not be taken to mean that the increased government spending which characterised post-war capitalism was without its importance or indeed its serious economic consequences. And this certainly holds true for arms spending. Our objections to the theories of permanent arms economy rest not on the proposition that arms spending is of no economic consequence but rather on the fact that first, in these theories arms spending is separated out from the nature of capitalism as a whole in the twentieth century (its drive to war, etc.) and secondly, these economic consequences are misunderstood, being viewed through Keynesian spectacles. Now there is no doubt that arms spending was one of the potent sources of the inflationary pressures which had become so acute by the 1970s. If we look at the nature of military spending in a little more detail, we can suppose that the government carries out military spending financed by an issue of paper. Certain capitalists, lacking profitable outlets for their capital in other (productive) spheres, take up this paper. With the loans the government purchases arms which, let us assume, are destroyed in use. (Even if the arms remain physically in existence they cannot, of course, be the source of surplus value, that is the means of repaying the bonds which have been issued.) Where is the wealth which the bond is supposed to represent? Marx called such capital fictitious capital. Trotsky explained the point at issue thus:

> When a government issues a loan for productive purposes, say for the Suez Canal, behind the particular government bond there is a real value. The Suez Canal provides passageway for ships, collects tolls, provides revenue, and in general participates in economic life. But when a government floats war loans, the values mobilised by these loans are subject to destruction, and in the process additional values are obliterated. Meanwhile the war bonds remain in the citizens' pockets and portfolios. The state owes hundreds of billions. These hundreds of billions exist as paper wealth in the pockets of those who made loans to the government. But where are the real billions? They no longer exist. They have been burned. They have been destroyed. What can the owner of these securities hope for? If he happens to be a Frenchman, he hopes that France will be able to wring billions out of German hides, and pay him. (Trotsky 1960: 185)

Here is the key to understanding one of the most powerful sources of inflation in the post-war period and in the twentieth century generally. For, as Trotsky points out, military expenditure involves the production of goods which, while they do not circulate within capitalist economy (and are therefore not commodities), do none the less generate revenues in the form of wages to those who produce them, profits to the firms who undertake their production, and interest to the *rentiers* who lent money to the state for such production. The effect is one tending to generate inflation.

But the effect on the capitalist system when the accumulation of paper claims takes the place of the accumulation of real capital are not confined to the stimulation of inflation. Real accumulation of capital (in short, capital which leads to the production–extraction of surplus value in industry) has a double effect. On the one hand it stimulates economic activity, raising the level of employment as more workers are drawn into work and raising incomes in line with the expansion of employment. On the other hand it leads to an enlargement of the capital of the owner concerned and provides the source for further productive investment. Now with regard to the accumulation of paper capital associated with the financing of a growing military budget, as we have noted in connection with government spending as a whole, the first effect is identical: the level of economic activity expands and along with it the level of income. A billion dollars spent by the state from loans stimulates business activity just as much as does the investment of a similar sum by the owner of capital in the expansion of his business. But there the analogy ceases. For after the fictitious investment, the wealth is gone and only the piece of paper remains. How is the government to make payment on it? By levying taxes? But as we know, this can only bite into the surplus value of the productive sector of the economy, slow down the rate of accumulation, and exacerbate the tendency for the rate of profit to fall. In other words, fictitious capital is not, from the point of view of capital as a whole, a real asset but a parasitic claim which fastens on to, lives off the back of, real capital. Its expansion, beyond a definite limit, must lead to an intensification of the struggle between classes as the owners of capital as a whole attempt to pass the burden of financing such spurious capital onto the working class (through reductions in living standards, efforts at greater exploitation, etc.) but also to the intensification of rivalries between the owners of capital as they strive to make sure 'others' will carry the burden.

One final point needs to be dealt with in concluding the discussion in this chapter. The idea that government spending is the root cause of the mounting capitalist crisis has been widespread in recent years, its most publicised representatives on the right being Bacon and Eltis. The thrust of this chapter is that state spending does indeed constitute a burden for capitalism, whether it be financed by an equivalent volume of taxation or by state borrowing. But to conclude from this that the capitalist crisis has been created by this government spending and that its reduction would re-establish stability would be to take a false step. As we have seen, the momentum of capital accumulation is determined above all by the rate of profit: as long as the rate of profit (or in some circumstances the mass of profit) is growing, a rising volume of state spending can be carried by capitalism without any necessary threat to its general stability. So the real source of the crisis must be located in the increasing difficulty which capitalism as a whole and especially its weaker sections experience in maintaining its rate of profit and this, for Marxism, is the classical expression of the fundamental contradiction of capitalism. Because of its political implications this point must be stressed, especially in connection with state spending on the social services. That capitalism is no longer able to finance an adequate welfare state, and is in fact driven to make severe cuts in this area, indicates not that spending on the welfare state is the cause of the crisis but signifies that capitalism can no longer provide the basic requirements (health care, education, social services, etc.) for the millions who are, after all, the most decisive element in the productive forces. The roots of this inability are to be found not in the national economy and its malfunctioning, but are international in character and it is to these international aspects of the crisis of Keynesianism that we now turn.

Notes

1. At one point Harman (1984: 81) says: 'Any honest empirical study of the 1940s, 1950s and early 1960s thus has to see that a historically high level of arms expenditure was accompanied by a stabilisation of the system, an offsetting of the tendencies for the organic composition of capital to rise and the rate of profit to fall, and a prolonged period of boom.' But matters can never be settled in this way: or rather for the empiricist only can they be so settled. The fact that arms expenditure increased and capitalism experienced a boom over a certain period cannot of itself establish that the boom was created by the spending on arms. And this is so no matter how 'honest' or detailed the facts gathered in support of the proposition. The same facts could just as readily support the conclusion that arms expenditure grew because an expanding capital could afford to make such outlays.

2. As we know, Marx opposed utopian socialists such as Weston because they denied that trade unions could exert any upward pressure on the level of wages. In periods of boom especially the working class may, for a more or less short period, be able to drive its wages up 'above value'. But the basic law remains: wages are the price of labour power.

3. Some such as Rowthorne hold that arms spending is important for capital in that it may generate technical change in the economy as a whole due to spin-off effects. This

is of course undoubtedly so. But the fact still remains that such expenditures constitute a deduction from surplus value and their (indirect) impact on the rest of the economy depends absolutely on the conditions for profitable production in the private sector of the economy. Unless those conditions prevail, state spending of whatever kind can have no impact, except a negative one. So it is on the conditions of production, the possibilities of and limits to profitable production, that the investigation of capitalist economy must centre. One further point in this connection. To the extent that arms production creates the conditions for technical change in other branches of the economy it must, via increases in the organic composition of capital, create downward pressures on the rate of profit. It might be said that arms production is 'necessary' for capital (as a means to war, etc.). But here again the economic impact of arms spending cannot be judged from this standpoint. Many things are absolutely necessary for capitalism (a state machine, for instance) which do not however create surplus value. The same point applies just as much to spending on the welfare state which, under certain conditions, capitalism may find it vital to make. This was obviously so during and after the Second World War when the proposals for the Welfare State were inspired by fear of the consequences of not providing certain minimum benefits for the working class in Britain. But again, this cannot be the basis on which we decide whether such spending was productive. Only that expenditure which leads to the creation of surplus value is productive. This is the essential point to be kept continually in mind.

4. Joan Robinson (1962: 96) appears to share this view, to some extent at any rate: 'Nowadays the paradoxes are taken in sober earnest and building weapons that become obsolete faster than they can be constructed has turned out far better than pyramids ever did to keep up profit without adding to wealth. The relapse on Wall Street that follows any symptom of relaxation in the Cold War is a clear demonstration of the correctness of Keynes' theory.'

5 THE COLLAPSE OF INTERNATIONAL KEYNESIANISM

In Washington Lord Halifax
Once whispered to Lord Keynes,
'It's true *they* have all the money-bags
But *we* have all the brains.'
(Gardner 1969: xvii)

In the last chapter we have suggested that the longevity of the post-war boom in Britain cannot be attributed to the operation of Keynesian policies but was produced by objective forces at work in the economy. Further, when traditional Keynesian policies to combat rising unemployment were attempted in the mid-1970s, they ran into the direct opposition of the International Monetary Fund. Bowing to this pressure, the then Labour government broke all the conventional Keynesian rules and began a deflation of the economy which has been followed by the Thatcher governments from 1979 onwards.

In one respect, however, it can still be argued that the 30 years or so which followed 1945 did constitute the Age of Keynes, if not on the level of the national economy then certainly on the plane of international economic relations. For these were the years in which the leading capitalist powers, led by the United States, attempted to establish a regulated international financial and economic order which would avoid the ravages of the 1930s and their attendant social and political implications. And although this order did not correspond to the exact pattern for which Keynes worked at the end of his life, it was none the less consonant with his general view: namely that appropriate state action, or in this case action by a number of states operating together, would be able to iron out the most violent amplitudes of the capitalist economic cycle. This new order was enshrined in the articles of the International Monetary Fund, brought into being as a result of the Bretton Woods conference which convened in 1944, with Keynes acting as chief British spokesman.

It was in a sense fitting that Keynes should assume this position, for one of the central issues which occupied him throughout his life was the struggle to fashion an international economic and financial framework in which British capital would be able to follow policies of its own choice. From his early concern with problems of Indian currency and finance, through his involvement in the controversies surrounding both the Versailles peace conference and the return to the Gold Standard in the 1920s, to his attempts at the end of his life to bring into being an international monetary order which would secure the survival of a chronically weak British capital, this was perhaps Keynes' central preoccupation. In this task he was of course grappling with two closely related issues: first, the fact that from the beginning of the present century the capitalist system as a whole was in historical decline and second, Britain's place as the leading industrial and financial power within this declining system had been taken over by American capital, whose unrivalled domination was so clearly visible at the Bretton Woods negotiations. An economic nationalist at heart, Keynes was at the same time forced to take cognisance of these fundamental and irreversible shifts in economic and political power which were characteristic of the present century.

The Gold Standard

This was no doubt a painful process given that Keynes had grown up in a world still dominated by British capitalism, even though that dominance was coming under increasing pressure from the time of his birth onwards. It was a world in which capital, both industrial and financial, had been accumulated in Britain for over two centuries and more, in which imperial markets still provided a sheltered outlet for anything British industry cared to churn out. Any malfunctioning of the economy, it was assumed, was due to internal rather than external factors. Long before he reached the end of his life Keynes realised that these conditions had disappeared, never to return. This was already evident to him in the 1920s; it was starkly obvious to many more as the Second World War came to an end. In a struggle to create a post-war financial system which would enable an enfeebled Britain to adjust without too much pain to its greatly reduced role in world politics and economics, he hoped to persuade the Americans to reflate the economy by means of an international clearing union. The Americans rightly believed that Keynes' version of the new economic order would keep demand for commodities too high (in the initial post-war period this was largely demand for American commodities), would inhibit the free flow of capital (again predominantly American capital), and would prevent the use of monetary controls as an instrument of short-term economic policy. So Keynes' plans ran up against the crude realities of American power, against which the intellect, even one nurtured at Eton, was no match.

From the 1920s onwards, Keynes, dissenting from the predominant opinion in the City of London, was an opponent of the restoration of the Gold Standard. He rightly sensed that there could in fact be no 'return to normalcy' as the more short-sighted elements in the British ruling class fondly hoped or imagined; furthermore, an attempt to re-establish the conditions of Edwardian England would be inimical to the interests of large industrial capital, heavily involved as it was in world trade. Any thought in 1944 that the conditions existing prior to 1914 could be brought back into being was even more ludicrous and lacking in historical sense.

In the minds of its advocates at least, the theory of the pre-1914 monetary order to which they looked back with such nostalgia was straightforward enough. The Gold Standard is generally reckoned to have come into being as a result of the Paris Conference of 1867. Under this system, gold was the only form of international money and at the same time the base of domestic money and credit creation. International trade imbalances would be automatically corrected. A country enjoying a trade surplus would experience an inflow of gold which would make necessary an expansion of the domestic money and credit supply. This would lead to rising prices and consequentially a relative loss of international competitiveness. In precisely the opposite manner, a country in deficit would suffer an outflow of specie, with a corresponding retraction of its money and credit supply, a fall in economic activity and a resultant pressure on its domestic price level. These forces, it was claimed, would bring an improvement in its competitive position.

This was the textbook version of the Gold Standard. Many observers believed that at last an ideal monetary system had been discovered: it was simple, smooth in operation, independent of the foolish actions of statesmen. As George Bernard Shaw put it: 'You have to choose [as a voter] between trusting to the natural stability of gold and the natural stability of the honesty and intelligence of members of the Government. And, with due respect for these gentlemen, I advise you, as long as the Capitalist system lasts, to vote for gold' (Quoted in Anikin 1983: 134–5).

But in fact the operation of the Gold Standard hardly accorded with this idealised picture. The theory was derived from the quantity theory of money as proposed by Hume and Ricardo as well as from the latter's theory of international trade — the theory of comparative advantage. One of the arbitrary assumptions on which the Ricardian theory was based was the tacit view that all nations were homogeneous; that is, at the same stage of development. The theory was also static, a fact indicated amongst other things by Ricardo's view that it was perfectly possible for countries to invert their specialisms. Both Smith and Ricardo wrote in the period prior to the introduction of mass production and the possibilities of taking advantage of the economies of scale. However realistic this particular assumption might have been for a part of the nineteenth century it was increasingly undermined by the penetration of mechanised forms of production into more and more areas of the economy. So also was shattered the notion that the international economy developed in a balanced, all-round manner. In fact the law of capitalist development moved in exactly the opposite direction — to an ever greater unevenness on a world scale, as those Marxists (Lenin, Bukharin, Hilferding, etc.) who studied those new economic phenomena emerging at the beginning of the present century saw. And this unevenness was closely related to the disproportionate development of industry, concentrated largely in Europe and North America on the one hand, and agriculture on the other.

The theory underpinning the supposed operation of the Gold Standard was also based on the proposition that all economic operations are responsive to movements in prices and/or interest rates. This was far from being the case. In its classical period (the last three decades of the nineteenth century) Britain was a considerable exporter of long-term capital. British capital was used extensively to develop the productive forces abroad and as a result income flowed back into London. These movements had a certain logic and relative independence of their own which cannot be explained in terms of the supposed operation of the Gold Standard, and are certainly not reducible to the latter.

Also questionable is the idea, fundamental to the conventional view of the Gold Standard's operation, that the inflow of precious metals into a country brings with it an increase in the money supply, and, following the principles of the quantity theory of money, that this increased supply is the source of a corresponding inflation of prices. As we have suggested earlier, Marx was strongly critical of this thesis: if the economic conditions of a country (in particular the value of total commodity circulation) does not require an increase in the supply of money, then nothing will bring about an increase in that supply. The gold imported into a country with a favourable balance of payments may simply lie in private hoards (that is, cease to act as money) or lie in the vaults of the Central Bank.

Additionally, even if the increased supply of gold does bring an increase in the supply of money (by no means an impossible outcome) this will not necessarily produce an increase in prices. The exact result will depend, argued Marx, on the particular phase of the economic cycle which the country concerned is experiencing. Prices usually rise in the upward phase of the cycle and fall in the downturn. So the impact of a change in the supply of money will depend on the concrete circumstances in which such a change takes place.

Most critically, in the actual development of capitalism, the establishment of conditions of relative equilibrium was achieved not in the smooth manner proposed by the apologists of the Gold Standard but through convulsions, more or less acute. The outflow of gold from a country was an indication of an acute crisis, and, although often the means for its intensification, not its initial cause. Under these conditions, the banks curtailed their loans; it was difficult to get money for payments due, and sections of capital (the weaker, usually more competitive sectors) were threatened with bankruptcy. Credit was undermined and everybody wanted gold, or credit money exchangeable for it. The result of such financial crises was the curtailing of production, rising unemployment, a fall in national income and a drop in wages.

The fact that the Gold Standard endured for the relatively long period that it did is explicable not in terms of any technical mechanism or intrinsic virtues it may have possessed, but solely by reference to the concrete conditions obtaining in the world economy at the end of the last century and beginning of this. Because of the great specific weight which British capital carried in the international economy she was able to impose on the rest of the world the rules which alone made the operation of the Gold Standard feasible. In other words, the foundation of the Gold Standard was the position of London as the unrivalled centre in world trade and finance.

That the Gold Standard of the nineteenth century had been sustained by definite conditions which disappeared in 1914 is confirmed by the fact that the restored Standard of the inter-war period was a pale reflection of its former self. The historical fate of the Gold Standard after the First World War is well known and can be told briefly. Britain, like all the major countries, practically abolished the Gold Standard during the First World War: sterling was no longer exchangeable for gold; now the state sought to bring all gold under its control. As a result sterling fell in relation both to the value of gold as well as all stable currencies. The City of London, dependent for its world position on a strong currency, refused to accept this and every effort was bent towards bringing back the conditions which obtained in 1914, against Keynes' advice. Under the supervision of Winston Churchill, restoration of the Gold Standard involved a savage deflation in order to force prices down, jack up the exchange rate and bring about an improvement in the external payments position. The cost, as Keynes had indeed warned, was a price level which made many British exports uncompetitive in world markets.

The weakness of the restored Standard can be seen in the fact that it could not re-establish the circulation of gold coin (specie). Gold was almost entirely removed from domestic circulation and concentrated in the hands of the state where it became world money, a universal means of payment in the international economy. This system, brought into being with such problems and sacrifices, could not endure for more than a few years. In the case of both Britain and France (where the Gold Standard lasted longest, being abandoned only in the mid-1930s) a so-called gold bullion standard operated: the Central Bank would only exchange bank notes for gold of a fixed weight. Small businesses, not to say individuals, had effectively lost the right to hold their assets in gold form.

An additional factor indicating the weakened nature of the new arrangements was the fact that whereas in the nineteenth century the pound sterling was in effect the only reserve currency, the inter-war period saw an increasing challenge by the US dollar to the former hegemony of sterling. In retrospect it is clear that the inter-war years were an interregnum in which sterling had been deposed but the dollar had yet finally to take its place.

In the case of Britain the partially restored Gold Standard lasted barely six years, collapsing in September 1931 under the pressure of the world financial crisis. In the case of the United States the abolition of dollar convertibility was one of the first measures taken under Roosevelt's New Deal at the start of 1933. France, the country *par excellence* of gold, was finally obliged to depart from the precious metal in the face of a massive flight of capital at the time of Blum's Popular Front government. The old system of fixed parities was destroyed. Currencies were allowed to 'float', just as they were to be allowed to float from the 1970s onwards. In the competition for markets, countries were prepared to let their currency drop, thereby cheapening their exports and raising the price of their imports. This was but another form of protectionism. It was against this beggar thy neighbour policy that many economists, notably the Keynesians, subsequently complained so bitterly. This was somewhat ironic in view of Keynes' own conversion to the camp of protectionism in the 1930s.

The Establishment of Bretton Woods and its Collapse

In the summer of 1944 the delegates of over 40 countries assembled in Bretton Woods in the United States for an international conference which was centrally concerned with a question which previously had hardly been considered: the setting-up of an international financial system aimed at regulating world monetary and credit relations. Dominating these deliberations was the memory of the inter-war period with its collapse of the Gold Standard, the competitive devaluation of currencies, the growth of a series of restrictions on international payments and trade, and the severe political and social problems which this economic crisis engendered. The underlying assumption of the conference was that these events had been triggered off by weaknesses in the monetary sphere. The fear of a renewal of similar upheavals in the period following the end of the war and the threat which such upheavals might entail for the future of capitalism itself were upmost in the mind of most delegates. The situation in France, Italy, Greece and elsewhere was already fraught with potential danger, and only the restoration of some economic stability in Western Europe seemed likely to avert grave social dangers for capital, even if such stability involved a temporary retreat on the part of the ruling class.

One of the basic aims of Bretton Woods was the introduction of a series of strict rules of behaviour which would, it was hoped, prevent unilateral devaluation of a currency without prior agreement of the Fund and at the same time abolish the restrictions on world trade which had been such a damaging feature of the years between the wars. Second, it was proposed to institute a system whereby countries with financial problems would have access to certain international credits so that they would avoid the need for rapid and savage deflation.

But this did not mean that there was ready agreement on the shape which the new economic order should take. Far from it. As has been widely noted, one of the most significant features of Bretton Woods was the sharp clash between what were then the two leading world economic powers, Britain and the United States. This clash took the form of acute differences between Keynes and Harry Dexter White. Keynes, recently elevated to the peerage, was by this time considered to be the leading figure in economics, the principal advocate of the state regulation of capitalist economy, and the outstanding authority in the fields of financial and economic policy. White, on the other hand, was not an academic but a practical economist, Assistant Secretary to the United States Treasury then responsible for international financial problems, and a follower of President Roosevelt and New Dealism.

Superficially, White and Keynes shared the same objective: to overcome the past weaknesses of the world monetary system and thus help create the conditions for a renewed growth of capitalism. But this seeming agreement obscured a fundamental difference in outlook between the two leading figures at Bretton Woods. For while White wished to see the dominant position of American capitalism confirmed in the post-war arrangements, Keynes, with equal determination, wished to salvage something in the world economy for the once all-powerful place for British capital. The struggle was however quite unequal. Britain had been irrevocably weakened by the slump and by the war itself which had amongst other things obliged her to realise a large slice of her overseas assets. Never again would sterling be able to look the dollar straight in the eye. Keynes' proposals were listened to with apparent respect but Whites's plan was the one adopted. Here was living refutation of Keynes' notion that ideas were more powerful than vested interests. That he experienced the refutation first hand only added to the irony.

What were these plans — both incidentally published in 1943 — advocated by the Americans on the one hand and the British on the other? The White plan called for a Stabilisation Fund and a Bank for Reconstruction. The Fund was to be available for short-term lending to countries in temporary balance of payments difficulties, in return for which the contributors to the Fund would relinquish a considerable amount of their sovereignty — they would lose their power to vary their exchange rates; all forms of exchange control would have to be got rid of; and each member would have to submit to Fund supervision over domestic economic policy. Morgenthau's objective, expressed in a letter to President Truman, was 'to move the financial center of the world from London and Wall Street to the United States Treasury' (Gardner 1980: 76). The real significant shift was to be away from London. The British understandably objected that the White plan was merely an attempt to restore arrangements similar to those prevailing under the Gold Standard with the significant difference that it would now be the Americans rather than the British who would exercise the right to interfere in the domestic policies of any other country. This they would do through their domination over the Fund's assets and their disbursement. As Keynes expressed it:

> Any accommodation we accept from the United States must be on our terms, not theirs. Recent discussion in the United States and evidence given before Congress made it quite clear that there are quarters in the United States intending to use the grant of post-war credits to us as an opportunity for imposing (entirely, of course, for our good) the American conception of the international economic system. (van Dormael 1978: 155)

What Keynes feared specifically about the American 'conception of the international economic system' was that it would involve the destruction of imperial preference, giving the Americans access to previously privileged British markets and areas for capital investment, a move which, through the abolition of exchange control, would prevent the sterling area balances held in London being used to buy American goods. In general his fears were well grounded.

In opposition to White, Keynes proposed the formation of a Clearing Union with $26 billion overdraft facilities (five times the sum envisaged by White) and these facilities were to be divided according to the shares of pre-war trade. The Americans wanted any facilities available to a country in trouble to be based not on their share of world trade prior to the war alone (this was Keynes' proposal and would have given Britain a position comparable to that of the United States) but also on their gold holdings and national income — a move designed greatly to enlarge the share of America. Under Keynes' envisaged plan balance of payments surpluses and deficits were to be expressed in *Bancor*, a new international unit of account. Again, White demurred: there was to be no new world currency; the dollar was to be imposed on the international economy as the principal reserve currency, supported by American gold and the general strength of her economy.

What Keynes aimed at was the ability of a country (he meant Britain) to pursue domestic expansionary policies without the fear of the international consequences. (As Lord Kahn put it, 'if Keynes can be said to have devoted his life to anything, it is to liberating internal policy from the dominance of external factors', quoted in Milos Keynes (ed.).) White summarised the differences between the Americans and the British in the following way:

> Those [British] views happen to be different from those that were held by the United States and those that were held by a good many other countries present at Bretton Woods. . . . The controversy stems from the issue as to what is the major role which the Fund and the Bank, and particularly the Fund, shall play. It has been our belief from the very beginning that the Fund constitutes a very powerful instrument for the co-ordination of monetary policies for the prevention of economic warfare and for an attempt to foster sound monetary policies throughout the world. The British view, in my judgement, was based more on the concept that the Fund should play a role somewhat similar to that indicated in the International Clearing Union, that the greater emphasis should be upon the provision of short-term credit, that it should provide the necessary funds whereby a country, when it felt the need for foreign exchange, would be able to acquire it. . . . They

believed that there should be as little discussion as possible on . . . the role of the Fund to determine whether or not policies pursued by any member governments were or were not in accord with certain principles. (van Dormael 1978: 299–300)

The debate between White and Keynes was unequal. Britain no longer 'conducted the international orchestra' (Keynes' phrase) as she had done in the previous century, nor could she ever hope to do so again. Despite Keynes' intellectual force the delegates at Bretton Woods accepted a plan based on the American proposals.

The main aim of the new system was to keep the advantages of the Gold Standard while getting rid of its supposed defects. The advantages of the old system were held to lie in the fact that it preserved stable ratios between the currencies, allowed their mutual convertibility, and ensured the free movement of commodities and capital. Great emphasis was placed on the discipline associated with the nineteenth-century Gold Standard: a country living above its means would lose gold and would take restrictive measures — it would deflate its economy and thereby re-establish external equilibrium. The flaws attaching to the Gold Standard were reckoned to be its inflexibility, the fact that it imposed deflation on debtor countries too soon and too often. And because those gathered at Bretton Woods were above all fearful of the political and social consequences which a post-war deflation would bring, this was considered to be the major defect of the pre-1914 system.

In short, Bretton Woods involved a policy of (controlled) inflation as a means of avoiding social upheaval. In this respect it was based upon 'international Keynesianism', but an international Keynesianism firmly in the control of America, rather than Britain. Here was an expression not of the vitality of capitalism but of its profound weakness, the fact that it felt unable, as the Second World War drew to a close, to confront the working class throughout Europe in the manner which it had felt able to do after the First World War.

The basic features of Bretton Woods were as follows:

1. All currencies were pegged to the dollar, and their exchange rate could only be altered by international agreement, in effect by agreement with the Americans. The dollar replaced sterling as the dominant currency, a point soon underscored when, in 1949, sterling was devalued from its initial parity of $4.03 to $2.80

2. The dollar was to be linked to gold by the American guarantee to purchase dollars throughout the world at a fixed rate of $35/1 oz fine gold. Thus was the dollar said to be 'as good as gold'; indeed some went

further, declaring that as dollar holdings, unlike gold, attracted a rate of interest, the American currency was in fact superior to gold. But this was a forlorn hope: the position of the dollar depended on the strength of American capitalism in world economy and far from being absolute this was strictly relative.

3. Under Bretton Woods a central pool of reserves was established, to be administered by the Fund, which would make loans available on a temporary basis to countries in balance of payments difficulties. Each country contributed according to an agreed scale, with the lion's share being put in by the Americans. In short the IMF was from the outset firmly under American control.

4. As one condition for their participation, the Americans insisted on trade liberalisation. Tariff barriers were to be run down, a move designed to facilitate the dominance of American capital in the markets of the world. As we have noted, Keynes rightly saw this as a frontal attack on what was left of the British empire and the privileges which it had afforded British capital.

But the opposition to the Gold Standard which was expressed at Bretton Woods apart, the place of the metal, far from being dispensed with had to be accorded a role in the new scheme of things, despite the fact that, as Keynes had said as early as 1924, the intention was to remove gold's formerly autocratic power and reduce it to the status of constitutional monarch. Gold was made the measure of the international value of monetary units: each country pledged to fix and preserve the gold content of its currency. Gold was also declared to be the major international reserve asset, the ultimate instrument for settling balance of payments deficits. In short, on the international plane certainly, capitalism proved unable to free itself of the barbarous relic.

But just as the Gold Standard of the nineteenth century had in reality operated on the basis of the strength of British capital, so the system emerging from Bretton Woods was only as stable as American capital. The dollar was the means by which all major currencies were linked to gold. Indeed, currencies were tied not immediately to gold, but to gold via the dollar. In other words, the central axis on which Bretton Woods turned was the gold content of the dollar, or the official dollar price of gold, for it was this which in effect measured the size of any country's balance of payments deficit. This dollar price of gold remained fixed — at $35/1 oz fine gold until 1971, and this was the 'constant' on which the stability of the world monetary system depended.

The prime concern of each country was the dollar parity of its currency, for on this depended the profitability of its exporting and importing activities as well as the results of other foreign economic activities. Because of its vast stockpile of gold, the Americans could freely exchange dollars for gold, at least for foreign governments and banks. This exchangeability of the dollar was the thread which tied the whole currency system to gold.

In the immediate years after 1945 gold continued to flow into the United States as it had done in the pre-war years. The financial collapse following the 1929 Wall Street crash had brought a flood of gold from Europe into the US reserves. In the years 1934–49 (the outbreak of the Korean War) the American gold reserve approximately trebled, rising from some $8 billion to over $24 billion (based on gold priced at $35/fine ounce). Not only did widespread fear of political and social unrest in Europe induce gold-holders to transfer their holdings to New York, as well as to return their capital to America, but this trend was encouraged by a consistently favourable US balance of payments position and increased gold-mining in America itself. To put these trends in some perspective: on the eve of the First World War the Americans held a little over a quarter of total world gold reserves, not much more than France and considerably less than the combined Anglo-French holding. This figure had risen to over half on the eve of the Second World War (and was to continue to increase during the war itself). Thus the widespread complaint of financiers in the 1920s that there was a severe gold shortage in fact missed the point. What was crucial was not so much the absolute amount of gold available for financial purposes but its unequal distribution: by the end of the 1920s some two-thirds of all available gold was concentrated in the hands of the Americans and the French.

The fact that gold continued to move into America in the early postwar period reflected the impoverished state of Europe and the fact that gold was the only available way of paying for American goods. By the end of 1949 the American gold-holding reached a record level of some 22,000 tons, equivalent to 70 per cent of the reserves of the entire capitalist world. (Britain's share at this time was roughly 6 per cent, with the countries which were later to constitute the European Economic Community holding even less between them.) From this point onwards the movement of gold to the United States ceased and soon began to move in the opposite direction — to such an extent that by the end of 1960 America's reserves of gold were down to under 16,000 tons (representing now only 44 per cent of total world holdings) and in 1972, when the Bretton Woods system had in effect collapsed, the US held under 9000 tons (21 per cent of total holdings). Along with this steady decline in the American gold-holding went the erosion of that other prop of the Bretton Woods system:

the fact that in the years immediately following 1945 America was the principal and often sole supplier of many vital commodities, especially raw materials.

Until the severing of the fixed gold/dollar link in 1971, the privileged position accorded the dollar at Bretton Woods provided the basis for the rapid expansion of capital exports from the United States in the post-war years. These exports fell under three broad heads:

1. First the Americans had to make considerable loans to a war-devastated Europe facing economic collapse and social tensions which threatened the very future of capitalism. First in the form of lend lease and then under the Marshall Plan (the so-called European Recovery Program) loans were granted to assist in the economic, social and political stabilisation of Western Europe.

2. The Americans were obliged to undertake responsibility for a large slice of European military expenditure. Such expenditure was not of course made because it was imagined that it might have a stabilising effect on capitalism (in the long term the contrary proved to be the case) but because imperialism was driven to prepare for the reassimilation of those territories over which it had lost control in 1917, losses which increased as a result of the westward march of the Soviet army at the end of the war. Military expenditure by America was also required for an intensifying struggle against the colonial and semi-colonial peoples; here the war in Vietnam (following the Korean War), which ended in ignominious defeat in 1975, was one of several decisive events undermining the position of American capital in world economy. Here the resistance of the masses in the colonial countries, whose struggle had been greatly stimulated by the war itself, was a potent factor throughout the post-war period in exacerbating the crisis and instability of world capital. In this respect, the nature of military expenditure furnishes yet another example of the sheer impossibility of drawing a rigid demarcation line between economics and politics after the manner of much orthodox social science.

3. Dollars also flooded into Europe as a result of the increasing penetration of American capital into Europe, often into its key and most advanced areas of industry and finance. This was the result of no abstract policy decision on the part of the American ruling class. As Marxists have always stressed, the export of capital is one of the decisive features of capitalism in the epoch of imperialism, one of the principal counteracting forces to the tendency of the rate of profit to fall. The American monopolies saw in Europe not merely an outlet for their goods but also a profitable field for the investment of surplus capital, where, in part because of the ravages of war, the possibilities for profit were much greater than they

were at home.

Needless to say, many superficial commentators saw in these developments only the strength of US capital. But they were in fact indications of the growing contradictions of capital on a world scale, pointers to the fact that the Americans would be unable to sustain for long a policy of 'international Keynesianism'. The fact is that throughout the post-war years labour productivity in the American economy was growing at only some quarter the rate as that in Japan and roughly half the rate as that in Western Europe. That much of this productivity increase was the result of American capital invested in these areas was but one expression of the contradictory nature of the post-war boom.

One manifestation of these developing contradictions was the emergence of the so-called 'liquidity crisis' which began increasingly to exercise the concern of politicians and financiers from the mid-1960s onwards. In the world of finance it is a well-known fact that it you owe somebody $10 and cannot pay you are at the mercy of your creditor; if on the other hand you owe him $10 billion he is in your hands. For capitalism this became the nub of the problem. By the end of 1967 the United States owed the rest of the world some $36 billion, of which about half was to other governments and Central Banks. By the start of the 1980s this figure had shot up to over $200 billion. Now these debts (those of America to the rest of the world) have a specific character. For they are at one and the same time debts but also monetary reserves, international means of payment accumulated by countries outside America. In the first 20 years after the war the reserve aspect of the dollar was to the forefront and the fact that these reserves were also debts which America owed tended to be lost sight of. But once the dollar holdings of non-American governments and institutions reached a critical level it was their quality as debts which became decisive. It was this transformation of reserves into debts which was the single most important feature of the growing monetary crisis and which more than anything served to undermine the Bretton Woods arrangements and along with them 'international Keynesianism'.

The US gold reserve was similar to that which any bank has to hold in order to meet the cash demands of its clients. In normal times, a bank can manage with fairly small reserves. It is only when, for whatever reason, confidence in the bank has been undermined and depositors begin to get worried about their money that the danger of a classic run on the bank is possible. Such a possibility was hardly present in the early phase of the post-war period. In 1950, for instance, the US gold reserve was some seven times greater than the dollar assets of foreign powers. By

1967 the danger signs were already looming when this figure had dropped to 78 per cent. By 1971 the figure had plunged to around one-fifth.
Here a critical moment had arrived, at which point the US closed its
doors. Possibility had been transformed into reality, as dialectics puts it.

One of the factors explaining the drain of gold from Fort Knox was
the policy of a number of governments, notably the French, who set out
on a conscious policy of transforming their reserves from dollars into
gold. From the end of the 1950s onwards, enjoying a certain revival in
her industries and experiencing an improvement in her balance of
payments, which previously had been characterised by chronic deficits,
France embarked on a course of action which in the decade following
the late 1950s saw the central gold reserve rise over tenfold. This policy
was given credence by the school of metalism (advocates of metal money)
led by Jacques Rueff. Anti-Keynesian in its general stance (here Keynes'
role at Versailles no doubt had a role to play), it favoured the preservation of free-market mechanisms of which the Gold Standard was supposed to be the epitome. That France should take the lead in the
accumulation of gold was not wholly accidental, nor merely the attach-
ment to what Keynesianism would regard as an obsolete economic doctrine. It reflected the historical peculiarities of French capital, the classic
country of the *rentier*: money capitalists living on the proceeds of loan
capital. The *rentier* is above all interested in stability, expecting as he
does the repayment of his loan, together with an appropriate amount of
interest. Gold is the most stable money form. Hence the decided anti-
Keynesian slant of much economics in France, one of the countries where
The General Theory made little impact at the time of its publication. By
making the dollar a reserve currency, American capital had gained for
itself a considerable advantage, for it was able to run a balance of payments
deficit over many years, settle this deficit in paper form and oblige other
countries to hold the paper as reserves. By handing over goods and accumulating paper money, the tendency towards inflation was stimulated.
The Americans, said the French, must be made to settle their debts in
gold; this would force them to bring their economy into order. De Gaulle
followed Rueff's advice and from the mid-1960s the French systematically
changed their dollar holdings for gold at the agreed rate of exchange —
$35 per ounce of gold. Only working balances were retained in dollar
form. And despite appeals by the Americans to the rest of the world not
to follow suit (appeals followed by threats and arm-twisting) they were
unable to staunch the flow and the dollar's link with gold was finally
broken with President Nixon's historic announcement on 15 August 1971.

America and World Economy

One of the striking features of the history of the world monetary system throughout the twentieth century is that capitalism has on the one hand been driven to try to free its system from the grip of Keynes' 'barbarous relic', gold, but has found this in practice to be quite impossible, certainly in the sphere of international economic relations. Here again is an expression of Keynes' failure to grasp the real nature of capitalist economy and specifically the role of money within it. That capitalism has proved unable to break free of the power of the precious metal is no accident, for it is in the sphere of world economic and financial relations that gold comes fully into its own as both the final means of payment and as the universally recognised social materialisation of wealth. Thus says Marx:

> Just as every country needs a reserve fund for its internal circulation, so, too, it requires one for external circulation. The functions of hoards, therefore, arise in part out of the function of money, as the medium of payment and home circulation and home payments, and in part out of its function as money of the world. For this latter function, the genuine money-commodity, actual gold and silver, is necessary. On that account, Sir James Steuart, in order to distinguish them from their purely local substitutes, calls gold and silver 'money of the world'. (I: 144)

It is in this sphere, as Marx notes a little earlier (ibid.: 142) that the real mode of existence of money 'adequately corresponds to its ideal concept'.

It has often been pointed out that the monetary system of capitalism in its hey-day was based on the strength of sterling. This was perfectly correct in that it was the position of British capital in world manufacturing and trade and the City of London in international financial matters which preserved a degree of stability in world economy prior to 1914. But gold still retained a pivotal place in the entire financial system and only within definite limits could sterling substitute for gold in the settlement of international payments. And those limits were fixed by no means by the ingenuity of politicians and financiers but by the strength of British capital. In short, the collapse of the Gold Standard in the last century was indicative of the decline of British capital in world economy and the inability of any other power at that period to take Britain's place. Only after the transfer of economic and financial power across the Atlantic during the 1930s and 1940s (a process which involved a series of convulsive economic, social and military shocks to capital) could America take on the British mantle.

We have several times drawn attention to the fact that orthodox thinking sees economic categories not as social relations but as things. This certainly extends to money which is regarded merely as a symbol, a name. But money, growing out of the needs of commodity production, is a higher, more intense, expression of the relations of this form of production. And just as, historically, money developed not within primitive communities but on their edge — in their relations with other communities — so the essence of money is made manifest in relations between states ('as international money the precious metals once again fulfil their original function of means of exchange: a function which like commodity exchange itself, originated at points of contact between different primitive communities and not in the interior of the communities' (Marx 1971: 149)).

As far as the domestic economy is concerned, it is perfectly possible for other forms of money, including paper, to replace gold. (The debasement of gold coins, their wearing-out through use in part renders them token money.) This Marx recognised. But in the sphere of world economy it is quite a different matter. Here it is not possible that the domestic money of any one country can permanently act as world money; nor, given the inter-state rivalries which characterise capitalism, is it possible to establish an artificial world credit money which will satisfy the needs of all states, the powerful and not so powerful. Keynes' proposal for such a currency, *Bancor*, never had a chance of acceptance. It is for these reasons that Marx's dictum, 'Gold and silver are not by nature money, but money consists by its nature of gold and silver' (I: 89), really comes into its own once money as world money is considered. Nature did not create money, just as it did not create the banker. But once money develops it is the natural qualities of gold — its durability, its easy divisibility, the possibility of transforming it from bullion to coin and vice versa, the fact that it is rarely found in the earth's crust and is therefore valuable, etc. — which render it more suitable than any other commodity for the role of the money commodity.

In the period after 1945 this appeared to be far from the case. This was an indication not that gold had been knocked off its pedestal but that appearances, as always, were deceptive. Marx used to remark with a certain irony that bourgeois economics were proud to have discovered that money was one commodity amongst many. This discovery was lost sight of as first gold was replaced in domestic circulation by paper and then, in the world sphere, the dollar dislodged, or promised to dislodge, gold from its premier position. The printing press, or the banker's pen, appeared to be able to create money and credit at will. Indeed, apart from one or two eccentrics such as Rueff and his fellow thinkers in France, it was fashionable to heap abuse on the gold currency system. But later developments established that those who derided gold, who along with Keynes considered it an outmoded relic, laughed a little prematurely. In the abuse of the Gold Standard was expressed not the wisdom of the economists but the fact that they were mocking something which intuitively they knew was no longer attainable. By subscribing to the notion that 'the dollar was as good as gold' the economists were in fact obscuring a fundamental contradiction of the post-war financial system which for the most part went unnoticed: the use of the currency of one country, America, as the credit money for the whole capitalist world.

Of course the denigration of gold, especially in periods of prosperity, is nothing new in the history of economics. Its roots lie in the one-sided rejection by classical economics of mercantilism and its doctrine that only the precious metals constituted real wealth. From the eighteenth century onwards economics moved to an extreme antithetical position: money was merely a conventional measure of price — a view which obscured its various other functions, notably as a means of holding wealth, that is as hoard.

Leaving aside for the moment the question of gold, there is no doubt that the stability of the world economy in the years after 1945 clearly rested on the power of American capital. The collapse of the Bretton Woods arrangements and the subsequent crisis testify to the fact that while American capitalism was undoubtedly powerful, the contradictions of world capitalism proved to be somewhat stronger. In other words, the strength of US capitalism was relative and never absolute. In the twentieth century Britain was replaced by America as the dominant economic and financial power just as the dollar replaced sterling as the principal form of world credit money. But precisely because America assumed her position in the period of the overall crisis of capitalism she proved unable to emulate Britain's position in the nineteenth century. To put the matter concretely, whereas Britain had sustained the development of capitalism in the last century by means of a surplus, America did so after 1945 from exactly the reverse position: on the basis of a growing balance of payments deficit.

This was an indication of the fact that America, for all her power, never carried the same weight in world economic and financial relations as had Britain in the nineteenth century. Whereas Britain had been able to dominate a world in which some countries were just embarking on the road to capitalist development (Germany, America herself, etc.) or who remained colonial or semi-colonial appendages (India, Argentina, etc.) this was far from being the case with the United States. As the economies of Western Europe expanded in the late 1940s through to the 1960s America found herself increasingly challenged from already mature capitalist countries, each with their own specific imperialist interests in world economy and politics. Despite the demagogic claims from some quarters, America was quite incapable of reducing the countries of Europe, Britain included, to colonial status. From the historical angle this was quite out of the question.

Looking more specifically at the matter, one important factor sustaining the Gold Standard of the last century lay in the fact that Britain's surplus on foreign account was largely self-sustaining. Because Britain was by far and away the dominant manufacturing power in a world consisting largely of commodity producers, her foreign loans — which expanded considerably after 1870 — were used by their recipients to purchase British goods. Second, Britain had direct political control over a vast colonial empire. India was of course the classic case. This allowed Britain not only to levy taxes from the empire but also meant that surpluses which were earned could be used to offset deficits Britain might incur as a result of the increasing export of capital — such an important feature of her economy in the latter part of the nineteenth century. As de Cecco (1974) has shown, Britain was able to square her accounts with the rest of the world in the period prior to 1914 principally because of her empire whose trade surpluses based on the export of primary products helped sustain a large outflow of British capital.

America was not afforded this luxury. Denied the possibility of direct taxation on an empire, at the same time she found that her export of capital tended not to build up trade surpluses but on the contrary laid the basis for increasingly successful challenges to her hegemony in world economy: West Germany and Japan were the most important instances of this phenomenon.

This has led some commentators to explain the current crisis of world economy in terms of the 'hegemony theory of stability' which argues that generally states are more likely to realise their common interests in a hegemonic structure dominated by a single state (see Odell (1982) for an example of this position). The American economist and economic historian, Kindleberger, holds a similar position, according to him,

The world economic system was unstable unless some country stabilised it, as Britain had done so in the nineteenth century up to 1913. In 1929, the British couldn't and the United States wouldn't. When every country turned to protect its national private interest, the world public interest went down the drain. (Kindleberger 1976: 32; see also Calleo in Skidelsky (ed.) 1977)

Kindleberger's argument is that British foreign investment after 1870 was counter-cyclical: it expanded when profit opportunities at home were poor and was reduced when the domestic economy was expanding rapidly. But an expansion at home stimulated the importation of more goods which naturally involved greater stimulus for foreign exporters. Kindleberger contrasts this situation with the position of America in the present century: here foreign and domestic investment have been positively correlated and as such have had a destabilising effect on world economy.

The problem with such theories is that they are in danger of remaining highly abstract. Britain was able to exercise the stabilising influence she did on world economy (this influence was in any case relative and never absolute) because of definite concrete conditions which lasted for a relatively short period in the last century. America was unable to carry this role into the present century exactly because those world conditions had altered fundamentally. The most dramatic change was that whereas in the period of British dominance capitalism was still expanding on a world scale, and rapidly so, in the present century the dominant tendency is towards stagnation such that any expansion in one sphere of world economy or by one country can only be at the expense of another sphere or country. The imperialist stage of capitalism is bound of necessity to find its acutest expression in the contradictions of the dominant capitalist power, America, and above all in her relations with world economy. Unless we start from these world economic conditions then any theory, including those based on hegemony, will remain devoid of real content. That is why Kindleberger, for example, can speak of 'the world public interest' about a system — world capitalism — which is in fact marked by ever sharper internecine conflicts between the various capitalist powers.

The fact is that the rapid expansion of world trade in the post-war years (which increased at a greater pace than did world production) was based on the dominant position of American capital in general and of the dollar in particular throughout the world economy. America was the main supplier of loan capital to the rest of the world — in the immediate post-war years virtually the sole source of such capital. But America played this role as an already mature capitalist country which, because of its 'over-ripeness', was impelled to export capital on an increasing scale, and this because of the lack of profitable opportunities for capital investments at home. The rest of the world, especially Europe, had little choice but to accept such capital exports in the form of the accumulation of ever greater dollar reserves. As we have seen, Bretton Woods involved a domestic money (or rather a token for money, the dollar) acting as the chief instrument of international payment. The dollar became world credit money. But the viability of this system rested on one vital base: the productivity of labour in the American economy, for it was this which in the last resort determined the stability of the dollar. As long as this productivity was developing at a sufficient rate, these world arrangements could be sustained. But in fact there were insuperable barriers to achieving the increases in the productivity of American labour. Not least was the fact that the capital invested abroad by American banks and firms was often in the most advanced sectors of the economy (petrochemicals, later electronics and computers, etc.) which did much to build up the position of America's rivals in world economy. Because of the wholesale destruction of the productive forces for which the war had been responsible, in many cases these countries (West Germany, Japan) had the advantage of starting with the most sophisticated technology as well as being able to employ a working class whose basic class organisations had been destroyed by the ravages of Fascism. Like Britain in the last century, they now enjoyed the advantages of being first.

But because of the privileged position given to America under Bretton Woods she was able to expand credit throughout the world on a scale far greater than was justified by the development of the productive forces in the United States (the index of which is the growing productivity of labour). Of key significance here was the mushrooming of the Eurodollar market. First established towards the end of the 1950s and comprising the dollar deposits in the European banks and American banks in Europe, this market amounted to around $2000 million in 1960 and had soared to around $60,000 million by the time Bretton Woods collapsed in the early 1970s. This was a measure of the debt built up by American capital, a debt which it had forced the Europeans to hold as reserves. Marx's comments on the role of the credit system have a strikingly contemporary ring:

If the credit system appears as the principal lever of overproduction and excessive speculation in commerce, this is simply because the reproduction process, which is elastic by nature, is now forced to its most extreme limit; and this is because a great part of the social capital is applied by those who are not its owners, and who therefore proceed quite unlike owners who, when they function themselves, anxiously weigh the limits of their private capital. This only goes to show how the valorisation of capital founded on the antithetical character of capitalist production permits actual free development only up to a certain point, which is constantly broken through by the credit system. The credit system hence accelerates the material development of the productive forces and the creation of the world market. . . . At the same time, credit accelerates the violent outbreaks of this contradiction, crises, and with these the elements of the dissolution of the old mode of production. (III: 431–2)

Given the fact that dollars piled up at a rate outside of the United States which was fundamentally out of line with the development of the American economy, the depreciation of the dollar was inevitable. In fact the dollar has been depreciating for much of the post-war years but this was a fact for a long period obscured by the artificial fixing of the dollar's price in terms of gold. Because the productivity of labour was increasing less rapidly in America than elsewhere, the American balance of trade, which in most years had shown a surplus, was turned into a deficit. It was these developments which finally led to the refusal of the Europeans and the rest of the capitalist world generally any longer to accept the dollar in the manner in which they had done throughout the 1950s and 1960s. The increasingly artificial dollar price of gold had to be abandoned in 1971. And with that abandonment the experiment in international Keynesianism effectively came to an end. All the old vices which it was thought had been eliminated by Bretton Woods returned as floating currencies replaced the system of pegged rates. The openly inflationary character of the dollar found its expression in explosive price increases, notably that of oil.

The Impact of 1971

In every sense of the word, 15 August 1971, when the dollar was finally revealed openly to be an inflationary form of credit money, marked a decisive point in the development of post-war capitalism. All the basic tendencies of the previous two decades or so were turned into their opposite: controlled inflation was now transformed into near uncontrolled inflation. Keynesianism was one of the principal casualties of this transformation.

The statistics of the period indicate the nature of this transformation. If the two decades 1960–69 and 1970–79 are compared, we find the following: whereas in the first period GDP grew at an annual average rate of 5.2 per cent, in the second period it was growing at only 3.3 per cent. If GDP per capita in the big capitalist countries is considered, this shows an even sharper slowdown: from a 4.1 per cent per annum rate of increase to 2.5 per cent in the second decade. Similarly with total industrial output. In the 1960s this was increasing at 9.5 per cent per annum; in the following decade the figure slumped to 3.6 per cent. The figures for energy production are even more dramatic: here, again taking the large capitalist economies, the expansion of energy production fell from its 1960 rate of 3.3 per cent to a mere 1.3 per cent in the 1960s. These developments inevitably hit world trade. Whereas in the 1960s imports into the major capitalist countries were growing at an average annual rate of 9 per cent, the figure fell away to 5.5 per cent. The corresponding figures for exports were 8.4 per cent and 6.5 per cent.

Not only this, but it was in the 1970s that the rate of inflation, as ever an expression of a basic disruption in world economy, began to accelerate sharply. Most dramatically affected were world commodity prices and most of all oil, the decisive energy source. The terms of trade (the ratio of export prices to import prices) turned markedly against the big capitalist countries in favour of the colonial and semi-colonial economies. Thus in 1951, in the middle of the Korean War, this ratio stood at 115 and fell steadily for the next 20 years to a figure of around 80 in 1970. It then shot up by almost 40 points to stand at 139 in 1974, with serious consequences for the balance of payments position of the countries of Western Europe and North America. Britain, traditionally reliant on cheap food imports, was especially hit by this shift in the terms of trade, and this trend was part of those forces which impelled in 1973 the bourgeoisie in Britain, albeit with much misgiving, into the Common Market.

As we have noted, although the Bretton Woods monetary system involved the creation of huge international debts based on the dollar as the principal world credit money, most of the major capitalist countries managed to keep their state debts under some degree of control in the post-war period. It was in the 1970s that public debt began to rise rapidly — in the case of Britain from a figure of some £34,630 million in 1972 to some £106,538 million by the end of the decade. The corresponding figures for the US show increases of a similar magnitude. The British government was now obliged to run ever greater budget deficits in order to try and keep the economy afloat and in particular to preserve the rate of profit on capital. In the decade up to 1981 the public sector borrowing requirement (the PSBR, now a key piece of jargon in economic discussions rose from a little over £2000 million in 1971 to over £10,000 million. Taking the years 1972–82 the total PSBR amounted to over £87,000 million. Here was a double-edged crisis. As we have seen, even if state spending is matched by an equivalent volume of taxation such spending still

constitutes a drain on surplus value. But now this problem was compound-
ed by the fact that an ever greater proportion of state spending was now
met out of loans and this was one of the principal factors serving to drive
up interest rates which in the case of Britain rose from a figure of some
7 per cent at the end of 1970 to around 14 per cent a decade later. Over
the same period the money supply in Britain increased by nearly 250
per cent and although the rate of increase was less dramatic in America,
even here the figure shot up by around 100 per cent over the same decade.

   These figures provide the background to the attack which was now
launched on state spending, especially in the sphere of health, education
and the other social services. This, as we have earlier stressed, arose
not on the basis of some abberant ideological quirk on the part of politicians such as Thatcher or Reagan but expressed the fact that in a period
of intensifying world slump such unproductive expenditure could no
longer be tolerated by capital. The extent of the problem created by the
long period of rising state expenditures is indicated by the American
figures which show that interest on the national debt in 1983 amounted
to some $90 billion and is projected to rise to some $116 billion in the
fiscal year 1985, equivalent to some 13 per cent of federal outlays.

   This mushrooming of internal debt is matched by an equally rapid
growth of debt on a world scale. Throughout the 1960s America continually exploited its privileged position in the sphere of international
monetary arrangements by issuing ever greater quantities of dollars which
had less and less gold backing. The great investment drive of the American
monopolies, the growth of 'aid' programmes with strict political strings
attached and rapidly increasing military expenditures were based on the
banks' seeming ability to create money and credit at the stroke of a pen
without any backing other than the credibility and political power of the
American state. It is the cumulation of these trends which has imposed
impossible levels of indebtedness on the colonial and semi-colonial countries, to the point where many of them are in effect bankrupt. The external debt paid by the colonial countries rose from its 1975 level of
approximately $180 billion to its 1982 year-end total of over $600 billion.
At present debt levels, per capita debt now stands at some $1000. The
World Bank has calculated that of every dollar loaned abroad in 1980
some 80 cents were required for debt servicing, and for every one percen-
tage increase in interest rates the colonial countries are obliged to find
an additional $13 billion.

   It goes without saying that the impact of the 'debt crisis' as it is known
cannot be confined to the colonial and semi-colonial economies.
Stimulated by the prospect of higher earnings resulting from increased

commodity prices after 1971, many private banks have become heavily involved in lending to the 'developing countries' over the last decade or so, to some extent replacing the official agencies (World Bank, etc.) in this role. The threat on the part of countries such as Bolivia, Ecuador and the Argentine to default on their foreign debts continues to have the most serious consequences for the viability of banks throughout Europe and North America. Several of these banks have been forced to declare many of their loans to such countries to be 'non-performing' which, from the point of view of capital, is an unsustainable position.

While it is of course not possible to predict the immediate course of events in all their empirical detail one thing is undeniable: the general trends in world economy are all too clear: towards greater protectionism and currency manipulation as each capitalist country seeks desperately to resolve its own crisis at the expense of its rivals. Even as this book is being completed, amidst ever more strident calls from sections of American industry for protectionist measures against Japanese and European industry, it is transparent that the major forces in world economy are heading for a return to the conditions of the 1930s, conditions which Keynesianism was supposed finally to have disposed of. This fact alone perhaps allows us to put Keynes' contribution to economic theory and policy into some perspective.

CONCLUSION

Needless to say, not all aspects of the crisis of Keynesianism have been considered in this book. Given its length this was not in any event possible. Concentration has been deliberately placed throughout on the fundamental methodological matters which are involved in a consideration of the nature of Keynesianism. The failure of Marxists in the past to deal adequately with these issues has been emphasised at several points. It is this failure, in the final analysis a reflection of theoretical scepticism, which has allowed those to emerge who wish to cull various bits and pieces from Marx in order to try to breathe life into a dying Keynesianism. This is not the first time this sort of thing has happened to Marx and doubtless it will not be the last. Such is the weakness of bourgeois thought as a whole that it is obliged to dip into Marx in order to provide a better antidote against him: ironical but true.

We have suggested that the method of Keynes was essentially that of empiricism, the outlook predominant in England. It was a method based on the acceptance of the immediate appearances of things as constituting the final arbiter of science. Marx proceeded from a quite different angle. And here, at the level of fundamental philosophical conceptions, involving basic questions in the theory of knowledge, there can be no bridges built, no compromises effected. Inspired by the task of preparing for the overthrow of the capitalist system, Marx's method was one which insisted on probing beyond these immediate appearances and thereby establishing the essence (a contradictory essence) of capitalist social relations. Only in this way would it be possible to establish both the necessity of the appearances of bourgeois economy and the historical necessity for their overthrow.

Now while the immediate appearances of the economy after 1945 seemed 'favourable' (rising output, increasing incomes and generally improving living standards) Keynesianism was accepted on the standard English grounds that it seemed to work; that it brought about desired results. As we have tried to show these appearances were in fact highly contradictory. In particular, they were far from being permanent, having been born out of the deepest social and economic crisis which capitalism had up to that point experienced. But just as the capitalist with a sum of money is little interested in the origin of his money (he is interested in expanding it, not ruminating on its source) so orthodox economics made little effort to probe to the historical roots of the inflationary boom which capitalism experienced from the end of the Second World War onwards.

It need not be stressed that the breakdown of Keynesianism has thrust orthodox economics into a deep crisis, perhaps as great as that which gave birth to *The General Theory*. Until recently at least monetarism seemed destined to replace Keynesianism as the new orthodoxy, although growing doubts as to its ability to 'work' have led an increasing number of economists to question its soundness. But in any event, whatever its immediate fate in academic and political circles, two features of monetarism are worth stressing. First, a point already made in the text: there is nothing at all new in this doctrine, and in this respect, orthodox economics is being forced to return to an old and discredited school as it seeks either explanation or rationalisation for the current crisis afflicting capitalism. Secondly, monetarism is based upon fundamentally the same empirical outlook as was the work of Keynes and his school. It too starts from the attempt to systematise the immediate appearances of the economy but just as little as Keynesianism is it able to inquire into the nature of such appearances, to penetrate to their essence.

We have earlier noted that Keynesianism, while badly bruised by the convulsions which hit world economy in the 1970s, is not completely dead. It still retains a certain degree of influence both amongst academics who continue to see it as the only viable alternative to monetarist doctrines as well as in the labour movement. We have not said a great deal about this latter question; our aim has been to focus on a number of theoretical and historical questions which in the long run are of greater significance. But the ability of British capital to reflate by means of greater government expenditure, if necessary behind a tariff wall, are bound to fail. As Keynes said, with 1914 Britain ceased to conduct the international orchestra. True then, it is infinitely more so some 70 years on when Britain's chronic decline as an industrial, commercial and financial power are patently obvious. Far from being able to pursue an independent economic policy, British capital is at the mercy of world forces over which she now has little or no control. And quite apart from the purely economic objections to be levelled at the feasibility of a Keynesian-style programme in current conditions, the reactionary political features which often accompany it are also worthy of note. As we have earlier suggested, the calls for import controls, exchange controls, etc. express the decay of capital, its inability to develop world economy, signify the fact that it is driven to turn its back on its conquests of the last century — free trade and an international division of labour.

Lenin was fond of remarking that in the realm of philosophy, when one form of idealism was in conflict with another, Marxism could only gain. This is certainly true of the present crisis of economics. It presents Marxism with a great opportunity to influence a new generation of students and others, increasingly restless at the inadequacy of the theories proffered by the various orthodox schools. But if there is to be a development of Marxism the fundamental philosophical and methodological issues which really lie at the root of bourgeois ideology in all its forms will have to be given central attention. It was as a contribution to that task that this book was written.

BIBLIOGRAPHY

Anikin, A. (1978) *The Yellow Devil*, Progress Publishers, Moscow

Balogh, T. (1971) *Labour and Inflation*, Fabian Society, London

Bannock, G., Baxter, R.E. and Rees, R. (1984) *Penguin Dictionary of Economics*, Penguin, Harmondsworth

Baran, P.A. and Sweezy, P.M. (1966) *Monopoly Capital*, Monthly Review Press, New York

Booth, A. (1983) 'The "Keynesian Revolution" in Economic Policy-Making', *EcHR* 2nd series, vol. XXXVI: 1 (February)

Briggs, A. (ed.) (1962) *Fabian Essays*, Allen & Unwin, London

Cairncross, A. (1978) 'Keynes and Planning', in Thirwall, A.P. (ed.), *Keynes and Laissez-Faire*, Macmillan, London

Carter, C.F. (1981) 'What is Wrong with Keynes?', Manchester Statistical Society, Manchester

de Cecco, M. (1974) *Money and Empire*, Basil Blackwell, Oxford

Dillard, D. (1942) 'Keynes and Proudhon', *Journal of Economic History*, 2: 1 (May)

Dobb, M.H. (1973) *Theories of Value and Distribution Since Adam Smith*, CUP, Cambridge

Eichner, A.S. (ed.) (1979) *A Guide to Post-Keynesian Economics*, Macmillan, London

Fetter, F.W. (1965) *The Development of British Monetary Orthodoxy*, Cambridge, Mass.

Fine, B. and Harris, L. (1976) 'State Expenditures in Advanced Capitalism: A Critique', *New Left Review*, 98

——— (1979) *Re-Reading 'Capital'*, Macmillan, London

Floud, R. and McCloskey, D. (eds) (1981) *The Economic History of Britain Since 1700*, vol. 2, CUP, Cambridge

Friedman, M. (1970) *The Counter-Revolution in Monetary Theory*, Institute of Economic Affairs, occasional paper 33, London

Galbraith, J.K. (1971) *A Contemporary Guide to Economics, Peace and Laughter*, André Deutsch, London

——— (1973) *Economics and the Public Purpose*, André Deutsch, London

Gardner, R.N. (1969) *Sterling–Dollar Diplomacy* (2nd edn), McGraw Hill, New York

Garvy, G. (1975) 'Keynes and the Economic Activists of Pre-Hitler Germany', *JPE*, 83 (January–June)

163

Gough, I. (1975) 'State Expenditure in Capitalism', *New Left Review*, 92

Hansen, A.H. (1964) *Business Cycles and National Income*, Allen & Unwin, London

Harcourt, G.C. (1969) 'Some Cambridge Controversies in the Theory of Capital', *Journal of Economic Literature*, 7 (2)

Harman, C. (1984) *Explaining the Crisis*, Bookmarks, London

Harris, N. (1983) *Of Bread and Guns*, Penguin, Harmondsworth

Hendry, D. and Ericsson 'Monetary Trends in the UK', Bank of England Panel Paper 22

Hicks, J.R. (1974) *The Crisis of Keynesian Economics*, Basil Blackwell, Oxford

Himmelweit, S. and Mohun, S. (1981) 'Real Abstractions and Anomalous Assumptions', in Steedman, I. (ed.), *The Value Controversy*, Verso, London

Hirsch, F. and Goldthorpe, J. (1978) *The Political Economy of Inflation*, Harvard University Press, Cambridge, Mass.

Hunt, E.K. (1979) *History of Economic Thought: A Critical Perspective*, Wadsworth Publishing Company, Belmont

Hutchison, T.W. (1968) *Economics and Economic Policy in Britain, 1946–66*, Allen & Unwin, London

—— (1978) *Revolutions and Progress in Economic Knowledge*, CUP, Cambridge

—— (1981) *The Politics and Philosophy of Economics*, Basil Blackwell, Oxford

Ilyenkov, E.V. (1982) *The Dialectics of the Abstract and the Concrete in Marx's 'Capital'*, Progress Publishers, Moscow

Kaldor, N. (1978) *Further Essays on Economic Theory*, Duckworth, London

Keynes, M. (ed.) (1975) *Essays on John Maynard Keynes*, Cambridge University Press, Cambridge

Kregel, J.A. (1975) *The Reconstruction of Political Economy* (2nd edn), Macmillan, London

Lafargue, P. (1975) *The Evolution of Private Property*, New Park, London

Lenin, V.I. (1969) *Selected Works*, Lawrence & Wishart, London

Leticke, J.M. (1971) 'Soviet Views on Keynes: a review article surveying the literature', *Journal of Economic Literature*, 9 (2)

Loadsby, B. (1976) *Choice, Uncertainty and Ignorance: An Inquiry into Economic Theory and the Practice of Decision-Making*, CUP, Cambridge

Marx, K. (1971) *A Contribution to the Critique of Political Economy*, Lawrence & Wishart, London

—— (1976) *Capital* vol. 1, Penguin, Harmondsworth

Marx, K. and Engels, F. (1956) *Selected Correspondence*, Foreign Languages Publishing House, Moscow

—— (1977) *Selected Writings* (in 3 vols), Foreign Languages Publishing House, Moscow

Mathews, R.C.O. (1968) 'Why Has Britain Had Full Employment Since The War?', *EJ*, vol. LXXVIII (September)

Mattick, P. (1969) *Marx and Keynes: The Limits of the Mixed Economy*, Merlin, London

—— (1978) *Economics and Politics in the Age of Inflation*, Merlin, London

—— (1981) *Economic Crisis and Crisis Theory*, Merlin, London

McLennan, G., Held, D. and Hall, S. (1984) *State and Society in Contemporary Britain*, Polity Press, Cambridge

Meek, R.L. (1967) *Economics and Ideology*, Chapman and Hall, London

Meltzer, A. (1981) 'Keynes' "General Theory": A Different Perspective', *JEL* (March)

Minsky, H.P. (1976) *John Maynard Keynes*, Columbia University Press, New York

Odell, J.S. (1982) 'Bretton Woods. International Political Disintegration: Implications for Monetary Diplomacy', in Lombra, R.E. and Witte, W.W. (eds), *Political Economy of International and Domestic Monetary Relations*, Iowa State University Press, Iowa

Pevsner, Y. (1982) *State Monopoly Capitalism and the Labour Theory of Value*, Progress Publishers, Moscow

Pilling, G. (1980) *Marx's 'Capital': Philosophy and Political Economy*, Routledge, London

Popper, K.R. (1947) *The Open Society and its Enemies*, Routledge and Kegan Paul, London

Robbins, L.C. (1932) *The Nature and Significance of Economic Science*, Macmillan, London

Robinson, J. (1951) *Collected Economic Papers*, vol. 1, Basil Blackwell, Oxford

—— (1960) *Exercises in Economic Analysis*, Macmillan, London

—— (1962) *Economic Philosophy*, Watts, London

—— (1971) 'The Measure of Capital: The End of Controversy', *EJ*, 81

—— (1972) 'The Second Crisis of Economic Theory', *AER*, LXIII (May)

—— (ed.) (1973) *After Keynes*, Basil Blackwell, Oxford

Roll, E. (1938) 'The Decline of Liberal Economics', *The Modern Quarterly*, I (1)

—— (1973) *History of Economic Thought*, Faber & Faber, London

Rosdolsky, R. (1977) *The Making of Marx's 'Capital'*, Pluto, London
Rubin, I.I. (1972) *Essays on Marx's Theory of Value*, Red & Black, Detroit
—— (1979) *A History of Economic Thought*, Ink Links, London
Schefold, B. (1980) 'The General Theory for a Totalitarian State? a note on Keynes' preface to the German edition of 1936', *Cambridge Journal of Economics*, 4 (2)
Schumpeter, J.A. (1952) *Ten Great Economists*, Allen & Unwin, London
—— (1963) *History of Economic Analysis*, Allen & Unwin London
Seligman, B.B. (1963) *Main Currents in Modern Economics*
Shackle, G.L.S. (1967) *The Years of High Theory: Invention and Tradition in Economic Thought 1926–39*, CUP, Cambridge
—— (1974) *Keynesian Kaleidics*, Edinburgh University Press, Edinburgh
Shemyatenkov, V. (1981) *The Enigma of Capital: A Marxist View*, Progress Publishers, Moscow
Skidelsky, R. (1975) *Oswald Mosley*, Macmillan, London
—— (1979) 'The Decline of Keynesian Politics', in Crouch, C. (ed.), *State and Economy in Contemporary Capitalism*, Croom Helm, London
—— (1983) *John Maynard Keynes: a biography*, Macmillan, London
Smith, A. (1976) *The Wealth of Nations*, ed. R.H. Campbell and A.S. Skinner, Clarendon Press, Oxford
Sraffa, P. (1960) *The Production of Commodities by Means of Commodities*, CUP, Cambridge
Strachey, J. (1938) 'Mr J.M. Keynes and the Falling Rate of Profit', *Modern Quarterly*, I (4)
Sweezy, P.M. (1946) *The Theory of Capitalist Development*, Dobson, London
Trotsky, L.D. (1960) *First Five Years of the Communist International*, vol. 1, New Park, London
Tsuru, S. (1968) 'Marx v. Keynes: The methodology of aggregates', in Horowitz, D. (ed.), *Marx and Modern Economics*, McGibbon & Kee, London
van Dormael, A. (1978) *Bretton Woods: Birth of a Monetary System*, Macmillan, London
Varga, Y. (1968) *Politico-Economic Problems of Capitalism*, Progress Publishers, Moscow
Weintraub, S. (ed.) (1979) *Modern Economics*, University of Pennsylvania Press, Philadelphia
Whillesley, C.R. and Wilson, J.S.G. (1968) (eds), *Essays in Money and*

Banking, in honour of R.S. Sayers, OUP, Oxford

Winch, D. (1972) *Economics and Policy: A Historical Survey*, Fontana, London

Yaffe, D.S. (1973) 'Crisis, Capital and the State', *Economy and Society*, 2 (2)

INDEX